CW00493930

Invasion And Deportation
- A Diary Of Euro 2000

JAMIE MASH
and
MATTHEW BAZELL

A Terrace Banter publication

Invasion And Deportation - A Diary Of Euro 2000 (Pbk)

ISBN 0 9535920 4 9

Published by Terrace Banter, Scotland
Printed by Heritage Press, England

Also by the same authors:

Toulouse Or Not Toulouse - Diary Of An England Football Fan by Jamie Mash (Janus Publishing, 1999)

A Terrace Banter publication from
S.T. Publishing
P.O. Box 12, Lockerbie, Dumfriesshire. DG11 3BW. Scotland.
www.terracebanter.com

Introduction

(Jamie)

EURO '96 HAD been a great few weeks of football, living the dream that England would be champions of Europe. So when the dream was suddenly shattered by a missed penalty against the bloody Germans, I immediately consoled myself by saying "bollocks to the European Championship, we're gonna win the World Cup". So for the next two years, I became more and more convinced that it was England's destiny to win the 1998 World Cup in France, and bring to an end what was now more than the 30 years of hurt committed to song.

Everything seemed to be going right for us. Glenn Hoddle was carrying on from where Terry Venables had left off, making England a team that could compete with the best. We won the Tournoi De France in July, 1997, beating Italy and France, and didn't concede a single goal away from home in the World Cup qualifiers. Even writing down the winners since 1966 seemed to be saying that it was England's fate to win the World Cup: 1966 - England, 1970 - Brazil, 1974 - Germany, 1978 - Argentina, 1982 - Italy, 1986 - Argentina, 1990 - Germany, 1994 - Brazil, 1998 - England?! (look at the pattern going either way from 1982!).

So after England drew 0-0 in Italy, we packed our bags and headed off to France with the army of St George for the 1998 World Cup. Optimism was sky high. Things started off well too with a 2-0 win over Tunisia in Marseille, although away from the field of dreams I got my head sunburned and the British press came out with the usual shite about us when the local Arab population decided to have a go. On to Toulouse and we had a great time there, but England fucked up and lost 2-1 to Romania. After three days and two matches in Paris, we went up to Lens for the Columbia game, got chased by riot police, and watched the match in a bar in another town. England won 2-0 to take us through to the second round against our old friends, Argentina.

After a weekend break away from the French in Amsterdam, it was down to St Etienne to watch the match in a bar. £200 a ticket? Fuck that! England played well, brilliant goal from Owen, but dodgy penalty, dodgy free kick, Beckham being a twat, Argie being a cheating twat, referee being a cunt, disallowed goal, missed penalty appeal, and then we were out after yet another penalty shoot out.

We were absolutely gutted, our dreams shattered yet again. But we'd been over there for three weeks and had had a great time, which eased the pain slightly until France won the bloody Cup!

Despite the heartache of our second round exit, our thoughts soon turned to Euro 2000. The draw for the qualifiers had been made in the Spring of 1998, we were up against Sweden, Poland (yet again!), Bulgaria and Luxemburg. The team that finished top of the group would qualify for the finals automatically, and the second placed team would go into the play-offs with eight of the other nine runners-up (the best runner-up would also qualify automatically). A draw would be made at the time to pair up the runners-up for a two-legged tie, with the four winners qualifying along with the joint hosts, Holland and Belgium, the nine group winners, and the best runner-up.

Sweden had reached the semi-finals of both the 1992 European Championships (which they hosted) and the 1994 World Cup in the USA, but had failed to qualify for Euro '96 and France '98, finishing behind Scotland in the qualifying group for the World Cup. I still picked them out as the main threat in the group though, especially as England always seem to struggle against Scandinavian teams.

I couldn't believe it that we ended up with Poland in our group again, having been drawn against them at least five times since we won the World Cup in 1966. They couldn't be seen as a big threat though, and I decided that I should go to the away fixture, having not been there before. I'd heard so much about the place from other people who had been there for previous England games that I wanted to sample it for myself.

Bulgaria weren't really a threat either, but couldn't be underestimated with players like Stoichkov and Lechkov in the team who had helped to famously defeat Germany in the 1994 World Cup quarter finals. And then there was Luxemburg who were just there to make up the numbers really. Their team consists of bank clerks, bakers, bus drivers and builders, so every team would expect to gain maximum points against them. Crap teams like Luxemburg, Moldova and Liechtenstein should be made to play in preliminary groups before playing with the bigger countries. That would help to reduce the size of the qualifying groups and avoid the need for such pointless fixtures.

So with the qualifying draw made, the fixtures arranged and the World Cup out of the way, it was time to focus our attention on qualifying for Euro 2000, and I started with the intention of going to at least half of England's matches, beginning in Stockholm . . .

Sweden away

(Jamie)

ENGLAND'S FIRST QUALIFYING game for Euro 2000 was a trip to Stockholm to take on Sweden, which meant we'd be getting our most difficult game out of the way. I wasn't planning to go there initially, but on the way back from France in the summer, we decided that it just had to done. There would be three of us going over to Sweden, me (aged 25 at the time), Matt (21) who's my cousin from London, an Arsenal fan, and of course co-author of this book, and Mel (21) from Brompton, Northallerton, who's a Darlington fan like me.

So, with my beloved Darlo off to a promising start to the season, it was time to head off abroad for another tour of duty with the army of St George. The match was on Saturday the 5th of September, and our journey started on the Thursday evening with a train down to London where we stayed at Matt's house for the night - after a few beers of course. Me, Mel and Matt got the tube to Heathrow the next morning and the Darlo-Gooner World Cup Party was reunited and raring to go!

Once we checked in for our flights, we we headed straight for the bar and a couple of pre-flight pints. It was the first time that Mel had flown, and I couldn't help repeating the lines from the film *Airplane*, when they're about to take off.

"Nervous?"

"Yes."

"First time?"

"No, I've been nervous lots of times."

It was funny at first, but after repeating it about a dozen times I think I did the other two's heads in! After a delay of about half an hour we were on the plane and up and away. The plane was fairly full and about half of those on board were England fans, so needless to say the beer ran out after an hour and we had to make do with wine for the rest of the flight. A lad from Millwall was sat behind us and he kept telling a Swedish lad next to him that "we're gonna do the Black Army", Stockholm's infamous skinheads who never seem to put in an appearance when England are there. We talked to the Millwall lad for a bit, and were soon at Arlanda Airport, Stockholm, greeting the plane's safe landing with a quick rendition of *The Great Escape*.

We got some funny looks from Swedes at the airport, as if to say, "Oh no, it's the English hooligans, ya." We soon got through customs, not forgetting the bloke looking at passports having a good laugh at Mel's photo ("This is you?!"), and then we got onto a bus that took us the 25 miles into the centre of Stockholm. We were dropped off at Central Station where we'd get a metro train down to where we were staying, a hotel right out in the suburbs to the south of the city. As we walked around Central Station, we were trying to work out which line to get, but didn't really give a fuck because we were too busy staring at all the gorgeous women around us. Swedish women seemed unreal, fucking beautiful, but we finally managed to focus on the task ahead and find our way to the right train.

We were on the metro for about half an hour before getting off at a station called Farsta, which was the nearest to our hotel. We then got a taxi to the hotel, which turned out to be another two miles away on the edge of a huge forest. Nice and scenic, but fuck all there. There wasn't even a bar, but after checking in, the receptionist sold us some bottles of beer which she had tucked away. We found a football outside and had a kick about for a bit, playing on until well after sunset, and on the way back inside the receptionist said that she'd give us a lift to a bar, which was appreciated.

After five minutes in the car, during which the receptionist told us that a load of Chelsea fans had stayed at the hotel in May for the European Cup Winners Cup Final, we arrived back in civilisation and were dropped off in Farsta to find a bar. This didn't take long and we were soon sat down drinking expensive Swedish beer (about £3.50 per half litre, which is nearly a pint). We were the only English in there, but we had no hassle, and the barman said that there had been some Birmingham City fans in during the afternoon. They must have headed off into the city centre, which we'd do the next day. After eating some pizzas, Mel got talking to a couple of blokes from Finland. There were right big fuckers and made us feel welcome by saying, "We're from Finland, we hate the fucking Swedish. . . if you fight tonight we fight with you, we back you up!"

So we spent the next few hours getting pissed with them and talking about England, Finland, Sweden and football. One of them challenged me to an arm wrestle and beat me easily, but then got beat by a Swedish bloke sat behind who looked a bit of a hard cunt. The Swedish arm wrestler's mate was a right mug though, looked like Geoffrey out of Rainbow, and said, "Tomorrow we fight, but tonight we are friends."

After he was seen slyly putting something in one of the Finnish bloke's drinks, I thought we'd be fighting sooner than he thought, but nothing kicked off. Some Swedes in the bar started singing, including a fucked up version of *The Great Escape*, so we responded with *God Save The Queen* and *No Surrender*. It was soon closing time and we left after saying goodbye to the two Finnish blokes and the barmaid called Petra, who was also from Finland.

We didn't really have a clue where we were and ended up walking down the main road, looking for a taxi to take us back to the hotel. Being pissed we soon got lost though, and ended up near the train station. Earlier in the day it held no worries, but by this time of night it had started to look like being a bit of a dodgy area.

Half a dozen Swedish lads suddenly appeared, came towards the three of us and shouted "Michael Owen's a wanker." I wasn't taking that shit from a bunch of Swedish teenagers, so I went towards them, fists clenched, hands to my side, and shouted, "Fucking Brolin's a wanker, come on!" They shit themselves and soon cleared off. Bunch of fannies.

Given the fact that we were in a shit area of a foreign city, the locals might have gone to find some of their mates, and there were only three of us, so we thought it'd be best to get back to the main road and head the other way. Luckily enough a taxi came along after a bit and took us back to the hotel. We had been walking in completely the wrong direction, but were soon back in our country retreat, looking forward to a day's drinking and the match the next day.

I felt a bit rough when I woke up, but was soon sorted out by the feast of a breakfast at the hotel. No fry up, but plenty of toast and bread with cheese, pate, and various cooked meats, all washed down with orange juice and coffee. Just what was needed to start the day. After that we phoned a taxi, which, surprisingly enough, was another Volvo, and got dropped off in the city centre, not too far from Central Station.

It was only about 11am and the match didn't kick off until 6pm, so we had loads of time to wander the streets, admire the women, drink beer, and do whatever else we could think of. There were quite a few other English about, and even in a crowded shopping street, we stand out a mile. The way we walk and the way we dress tells the world that we're English, even without wearing England colours. After wandering about, looking in the odd shop, and signing a petition against Sweden joining the European single currency, we finally decided it was time to start drinking. After all, it was nearly

7

1pm, and an Englishman can only last for so long abroad without a beer!

The first bar that we went in was down a narrow pedestrianised side street, with tables lined up along the outside. We got the beers in and sat outside, along with a few other English who were at the other tables. Numerous people came and went as we were sat there, but one in particular had us all in hysterics! Everyone was having their own conversations when it suddenly went quiet. A fat as fuck Swedish bloke with a very red and inflated face was walking up the street, wearing some sort of army uniform, carrying a small kit bag and looking completely fucked. If he was representative of Sweden's army, it's no wonder that they stayed neutral during the Second World War! He looked like the fucking Michelin Man in green!

The people at the end table started laughing, then we started laughing, then the next table and then the next, the laughter spreading like a domino effect, until the 20 or so of us English sat outside the bar were laughing like fuck. God knows what the Swedish Michelin Man felt like, but we didn't stop laughing for about five minutes, and even then someone would start chuckling away again. It was one of those moments where you just had to be there!

After a few more beers, we headed off down the road and stopped at a bar just before the main river. There were a few more English in there and the place sold a decent selection of food, so we had some lunch and a couple of beers before heading off for another wander, this time following the river for a while. There wasn't much down there, apart from a rebuilt Viking longship which we had a quick look at, but we eventually came to a large open area where there was a free blues concert going on courtesy of the local communist party. Even though it was all sung in Swedish, the music wasn't too bad, so we stayed around there for a bit. We got talking to a bunch of lads from Surrey, Essex and other Southern counties who now all lived in either Sweden or Holland. They were all in their late teens or early twenties and mostly supported West Ham, but a couple of them were as irritating as fuck. They were mostly a good laugh though so we stayed with them and after a while headed off towards Solna, where the Rasunda Stadium is, the plan being to have a few beers in a bar a couple of stops before Solna. One of the lads lived in Stockholm and had a Swedish mate with him, and they said that the bar would be full of English.

We got to the bar and it was indeed packed full of other English, with a few St George's flags tied up around the place. We soon got the beers in and stayed there for a couple of hours. I have to say that the place reminded me of The Globe pub in Baker Street, London, before an England match at Wembley. It was a good laugh in there, and at one point we got talking to a Swedish bloke that one of the West Ham lads who lived in Stockholm knew. He loved England and Nottingham Forest, wore an England shirt under his Sweden shirt, and called a Derby fan a sheepshagger!

After the pub we headed for the match, stopping off at a shop before the metro station where Mel bought three different Swedish chocolate bars, which were called "Kak", "Plop" and "Mot Creme"! There were a few other English on the train and at the Solna metro station, so we had a good sing song going up the escalator, *Rule Britannia* and all the rest. We were soon at the stadium, stood around for a bit and then went in, and had to climb at least a dozen flights of stairs to get to our section. It was the same stadium that England played at in Euro '92, when Sweden beat us 2-1 to knock us out of the tournament (Brolin, the wanker!), and since then they'd built another tier onto the stand that we were in, hence the lung-fucking climb. We just hoped that the scoreline wouldn't be repeated.

Once we got to the top we walked out into the stand and straight away we saw a familiar face. It was Hollis from Wolverhampton who we'd met in Marseille during the summer and kept bumping into, first in Toulouse and then in Arras, where we watched the Columbia match. We had a feeling that we'd see him in Sweden. After putting up our two Darlo flags at the back of the stand because there was no room elsewhere, we rejoined Hollis who was with Kerry, his wife to be. It was good to see him again and talk about the good times we'd had in France.

There was still some time go to before kick-off, so we got some beers from inside the stand. There were plenty of English in the stadium. As well as the main enclosure where we were, there were others below in the Sweden section, quite a few in the stand to the right, and a few scattered all around the other parts of the ground, including the opposite end behind the goal where there was a massive Doncaster Rovers Union Jack tied up.

The teams came out, followed by the national anthems, with *God Save The Queen* being sung with the usual pride and passion by the England following. The team got off to a flyer, winning a free kick just outside the area in front of us, which Alan Shearer stepped up to take and blasted it straight into the top corner. 1-0 after two minutes, time to go mental! England carried on playing quite well, we were making plenty of noise, especially with us all singing along to *The Great Escape* being played by the England Supporters Band, and it seemed as if it could only get better.

In the stand down below, which was mainly full of Swedes, some wanker was wearing an Argentina top and even had an Argie flag tied up on the fence. Not very clever when there's 4,000 English in the tier above, after them wankers cheated us out of two World Cups and had a go at the Falkland Islands in 1982. There was an English lad sat near him who decided to have a go at the Argie when he started mouthing off a bit, which became great entertainment for us lot up above. I think he was on his own or something because he didn't really seem too confident, waiting until there was a load of coppers behind him before hitting the Argie bastard. They dragged him off straight away, and after several plastic beer glasses and a shit load of spit was aimed at the Argie, he took down the flag, took his Argie shirt off and kept his head down. He wouldn't have lasted long if he was seen later on wearing that shite.

After that bit of entertainment, our attention again focused upon the match itself, which suddenly took a turn for the worse. Two goals in two minutes from Sweden and we were 2-1 down. England were suddenly playing like they didn't have a clue. It was bad enough when Sweden equalised, but when the second goal went in we were so fucked off, that the Swedes below us suddenly found themselves being covered in beer, spit, cigarette ends, plastic glasses and anything else people could get hold of. Someone even pissed in an empty plastic beer glass and gave the Swedes below a golden shower! I bet they were pissed off at that!

Not much else happened in the first half, apart from Henrik Larsson getting booed every time he got the ball, not because he's black but because he plays for Celtic, the fenian bastard. The fucking Italian referee thought it was racist abuse and the FA later got fined. What bollocks, it was political abuse, and he would've got the same treatment if he was white. No one likes Celtic because of their strong links with the Nationalists in Northern Ireland.

After half-time the match got even worse, with Paul Ince getting sent off for doing a stupid tackle. We did improve a bit later on and created the odd chance, but never managed to score and it stayed 2-1. Bollocks! After things looking promising to begin with, we'd got off to a losing start in our qualifying group, leaving us to play catch up with Sweden. This was made worse by the fact that only the top team would go through to Euro 2000 automatically, with the second placed team going into a two-legged play-off with another runner up.

We'd been told over the tannoy system that we would all be kept in for 15 minutes after the final whistle, but we were that fucked off we just wanted to get out of there and get pissed. The corridor in the back of the stand was about ten yards wide, with glass all along the outside. Blocking our way to the exit via the stairs were loads of riot police, looking ready for action with their shields and batons at the ready. I didn't see how it started, but all of a sudden something had kicked off and the police were getting pelted with anything people could get hold of. Signs for the toilets and other areas were quite a popular choice once they'd been pulled off, then a few lads managed to get a door off its hinges and throw that at the police. They kept threatening to charge us, but kept a space in between and then fired a few tear gas canisters. That's really clever in a confined space, so not surprisingly, after backing off a bit, people's attention turned towards the windows, with at least a dozen being put through, the glass falling about 50 feet to the ground below.

The police outside had cleared the area immediately below the stand, but beyond that there were loads of Swedes stood around watching us and taunting us. The police should've just moved them on and let us out. Seeing them wankers outside got me fucking wound up. After something of a stand off inside the stand, we suddenly realised that we could get out through the exit at the other end, so we just walked straight out, no hassle at all.

Once outside we could see back up to where we had been, and there were only about 20 lads left up there. After they'd chucked a coffee machine out of a smashed window to the ground below, the police made their move and nicked most of those still there. Nothing was going off outside, so we slowly made our way to the metro station, closely watched by the endless lines of riot police. They'd been fine up until then, but after that little incident they'd be taking a heavy handed approach to anyone they thought was stepping out of line.

We'd lost Hollis and Kerry by this stage, so the three of us went for the metro by ourselves, although there was loads of other English about. As we were going down the escalator we heard a load of Swedish starting to sing behind us, so we started singing "En-ger-land, En-ger-land, En-ger-land . . . ", but someone behind us said to keep quiet and to wait for the Swedish at the bottom of the escalator. We waited around at the bottom, waiting for it to go off, but there was police everywhere and nothing happened. With riot police all along the platform it would have taken a right fucking idiot to start something down there, and sure enough, some lad punched a Swede and was nicked in less than two seconds.

We got on the metro and found that there were Swedish fans all around us. Nothing happened though, and we were soon back at Central Station where we got off and went looking for a decent bar. We managed to find Hollis and Kerry again as we were walking out of the station, so the five of us went to a bar that was packed full of England and had about 200 riot police lined up opposite. We half expected something to go off outside, but nothing did and everyone was quite happy to find a seat and get pissed. After a couple of enjoyable hours in there, we headed off back to Central Station after stopping to get some food. Hollis and Kerry didn't have any accommodation for the night after leaving their bags at the station earlier on, so we said they could crash out in one of our rooms. After a half hour wait for the train, half an hour on the train, and half an hour walking, we got a taxi back to the hotel and crashed out for the night.

We had an early start in the morning, as our flight was at 10.45am and we had to check in at least an hour beforehand, so after a quick breakfast we got a taxi up to Central Station where we got the bus back up to Arlanda airport. We got there in plenty of time, checked in, had a coffee and then sat by the departure gate. Live entertainment was provided by one lad puking his guts up in the adjacent toilets, making so much noise that everyone sat around heard him and burst out laughing at every shout of Hughie! When he finally finished and came out of the toilet he got a big round of applause from everyone.

We were soon on the plane and heading back to good old Blighty, flying over a couple of football grounds (Loftus Road and Griffin Park) before landing at Heathrow. Good news when we got there - a quick check of the Sunday papers told us that Darlo had won 1-0 at Mansfield and were up to 6th position in the table. After a boring hour long tube journey to Kings Cross, we had a couple of hours in the Duke Of York pub, which I'm told has now been renamed and turned into some sort of poncey Australian theme bar. Fucking London and its poncey theme bars! The Duke Of York had become our regular pub in London, where we'd always stop off when Darlo played down there. Now it's just like most of the places in the West End. Anyway, after a few beers in there and a trip to the off-licence, we said goodbye to Matt and got the train back up to Northallerton, completing another trip away with England. Shit result, but we'd had a fucking great weekend. Luxemburg next.

Luxemburg away

(Jamie)

AFTER THE DEFEAT against Sweden in our opening match, it was essential that we got six points and plenty of goals in our next two games, at home to Bulgaria and away to the part timers of Luxemburg. Both would be played in the space of five days, and although I didn't go to Wembley, me and Mel were booked on a bus trip to Luxemburg, leaving on the Tuesday night before the match.

The Saturday got off to a good start as far as we were concerned. Darlo's match with Peterborough was changed to a 1pm kick-off, so a few of us got the early train up from Northallerton, had a few beers in the Speedwell (our usual pub in Darlington before matches), watched us easily beat The Posh 3-0, and then rushed back to the Speedwell to watch the England match. It was fairly packed in there, but there's a big screen as well as other TVs almost everywhere you look so there was no problem with seeing the match. It might have been better if we couldn't see it though, because England played shit and only managed a 0-0 draw. Fair enough, Bulgaria reached the 1994 World Cup semi-finals and still had a couple of decent players, but we should be beating teams like that no problem, especially at home.

Pressure was already mounting on Glenn Hoddle, with his criticism of certain players in his World Cup diary book, our early exit from the World Cup, and our opening game defeat in Sweden, but after the 0-0 draw with Bulgaria the press were really getting stuck into him. I've never been one for slagging off managers too much, and the way that England managers are treated by the British press is often well out of order, but then having said that, "England expects", and the manager is paid a shit load of money to bring success to a nation of 92 professional football clubs and nearly 50 million people. With the way we'd started our qualifying campaign for Euro 2000, even I was losing faith with Glenn Hoddle. Only a convincing victory in Luxemburg would ease the pressure on him.

Our trip started with a drive down the A1 to Ferrybridge Services near Pontefract, West Yorkshire, where the bus picked us up shortly before 10pm. It was only a £5 charge to leave the car there for a couple of days, and it was easier to do that than go to the next nearest pick up point, Hull. The bus was about a third full when we got on, having already been to Hull, and our next stop was Sheffield, where about 15-20 lads got on, all Sheffield United followers, who together with Hull City, made up the majority of those on board.

So with the bus just about full, we drove through the night down to Dover for the ferry to Calais. On the way down we put on the *Teargas And Tantrums* video, which is a video diary of France '98 by Eddy Brimson, who's from Watford and has also written a few books. It brought back memories for a few of us, and the scenes on the beach in Marseille when it kicked off with the Tunisians showed what shite our journalists were writing, but in the end we all got a bit sick of Eddy Brimson's face constantly saying, "It's a little bit naughty", or "They're having it large". It kept us occupied for a bit though.

We had a quick stop at Watford Gap Services on the M1 to pick up a few others, and I also saw Baggy, another Darlo fan who was on one of the other coaches, which we later found out broke down in Kent and they all had to get the train to Luxemburg. What a fucker!

After about an hour's kip on the bus, we finally arrived at Dover with about half an hour to spare before we had to board the ferry, so we all headed off to the Granada Services there, which, luckily for us, had a bar which is open 24 hours a day! Five o' clock in the morning, a pint of lager for breakfast! Fucking lovely. It was soon time to board the ferry and the bar. Suffering from lack of sleep (maximum one hour), and given the fact that it was still not 6am, and the sea was as rough as fuck, I'm ashamed to say that me and Mel only managed one pint each on the ferry. Still, plenty more time for drinking later. Just to give me a good beer base in my stomach, I went and had a fried breakfast before leaving the ferry. Tasted shit, but it did the job.

We were soon in France and on the coach, but before we got going we stopped off at a cash and carry to get stocked up on booze for the journey. Me, Mel and one of the lads from Sheffield got a couple of boxes of Stella Artois between us, just to keep us going for the five hour journey to Luxemburg. And then we were on our way, driving through France and then Belgium, drinking away, with two St George's flags (Darlington and Hull City) and one white ensign (Sheffield United) tied up against the windows to show Europe that we're English and proud of it!

People kept dozing off on the bus, but soon woke up when one of the drivers put a German porno video on! Going past a small convoy of lorries, one driver looked quite shocked to see a bus full of English lads going past, complete with flags, beer and porno. He must have radioed ahead to the next lorry because the driver was already

14

looking at the screens as soon as he could get a view inside the bus! Seemed to like our choice of video anyway. I dozed off again in between bottles of beer, but was woken up by the sound of what I thought was running water. But when I opened my eyes and looked at the TV screen, I was greeted by the sight of a woman pissing in a bloke's face. He was lapping up her piss and saying "Ja, super!" Fucking disgusting!

Once the porn film had finished it wasn't too long before we reached the Luxemburg border, and the piss hole of a country that is so shit and pathetic it's no wonder that they love everything that comes out of the arse of the shitty European Union! Our bus was pulled over along with every other English vehicle, to be checked by the police and military. They were probably a bit paranoid after the place got trashed when England last played there in 1983. At this point, one of the Sheffield lot, Harry I think his name was, took great delight in shouting, "For you, zie war ist over. Your hut ist second left, third reich!"

The police that came onto our bus to check passports must have been cadets or something. They looked like they should have been at school, but here they were, guns in their holsters, checking the passports of a bus load of England fans. After about half an hour, we were on our way again and into the outskirts of Luxemburg City. At this point, me and the Blades fan sat next to me whistled our way through our repertoire of war film theme tunes, including *The Great Escape*, *The Longest Day*, *The Guns Of Navarone*, *Colonel Bogey*, and *633 Squadron*. We settled on *The Longest Day* and whistled this for about ten minutes, before he started singing the words (which I didn't know at the time):

"Many men, came here as soldiers,
Many men, will pass this way,
Many men, will count the hours,
As they live the longest day . . . "

Kept us amused for the remainder of the journey anyway, which was only about 20 minutes.

Once we arrived in the city centre, we were dropped off near the train station and were led to our hotel, which was only about five minutes walk away. We checked in, dumped our bags, and then headed off in search of beer. It was only about midday, so we still had over eight hours until the match kicked off at 8.30pm local time. Everyone went off in their own groups, and me and Mel went from pub to pub with the Sheffield lot for some of the time, and had some food at McDonalds before going back to another pub. One place near the hotel was full of fucked up smack heads, so we didn't stay there for too long. By mid afternoon we headed up towards the stadium, stopping at a bar before we got there which had a few other English in, singing *No Surrender*.

On the way up there, as we walked through a bus stop area, a couple of local kids in their early teens noticed us walking past, and seeing the flag of St George hanging out of my coat pocket, they stopped their conversation, and one said, "Hooligan", in the irritating as fuck way that foreigners do. I immediately turned my head in their direction, shouted "Fuck off!", and carried on walking, which to them probably proved their point! Wankers.

We had a few beers in the bar near the stadium, and by this time it was pissing down, which is quite unfortunate when you're going to a shit football ground that would be a piss take in the Third Division, with no roof except over one stand. How they call that their national stadium, I don't know. I suppose it sums up their country - small and shite.

We'd got there quite early to put the flags in a good place, so once we'd done that we had two hours to stand around and get wet, with the rain getting worse. With no roof for cover, we found ourselves with about 50 others stood about in the toilet area, which at least was undercover. The rain died down though as the ground filled up and kick-off time approached. There was the usual variety of flags on show, but the best positioned one was the Doncaster Rovers Union Jack tied to the flag pole and hoisted up behind us. Could've been the same one we'd seen in Sweden.

We had some pre-match entertainment from outside when a few hundred ticketless England fans attempted to charge through the barriers. I think a few of them made it through, outwitting the riot police who were shitting themselves.

The match was soon underway and England got off to an average start, with one or two promising runs, but nothing special. After ten minutes though, everyone was stunned when Luxemburg were awarded a penalty. "The words 'San Marino' spring to mind," I said, referring to our 7-1 win over there in 1993 when they took the lead after ten seconds! I couldn't believe it though, we were going to go 1-0 down to a bunch of part-timers. This really was the low point of Hoddle's reign as England manager.

Fortunately though, the penalty was missed and it was still 0-0. Ten minutes later Michael Owen puts us 1-0 up to give us something to cheer about. We were all expecting the proverbial floodgates to open after that, especially when Alan Shearer scored from a penalty to make it 2-0. It never happened though, and at half time, despite creating a few more chances, it was still 2-0.

Once the second half was underway, instead of the goals we were expecting, we got a shit performance from a bunch of players who looked like they didn't give a fuck, led by a manager who seemed to be losing his mind with every comment and tactical decision he made. We tried our best to get behind the team, constantly singing *The Great Escape* tune for a while, but the players didn't respond. The singing then turned to humorous digs at Hoddle. First there was a version of the old 1970 unofficial World Cup song, We're On The Ball, which was featured on Chris Evans' TV programme, *TFI Friday*, before the 1998 World Cup, and mainly goes "We're on the ball, we're on the ball, we're on the ball . . . " for ages and ages. The version sung in Luxemburg was "With Glenn Hoddle, we'll win fuck all, with Glenn Hoddle, we'll win fuck all . . . "

Next was a song to the tune of "You're shit, and you know you are" / "Stand up if you hate Pooly" / "1-0, to the Darlington" (or *Go West* if you know nothing about football!). This one referred to Eileen Drewery, the faith healer that Glenn Hoddle employed as an essential part of his back room team, and went "Eileen, takes it up the arse, Eileen, takes it up the arse . . . " It started off round to the side, and when we could make out what everyone was singing, everyone laughed before joining in. Must have been the loudest song of the night, and Hoddle must have heard it.

Just before the end of the match, when it was still 2-0, we all sang (to the tune of *Blue Moon*), "2-0, we beat the bank clerks 2-0, we beat the bank clerks 2-0, we beat the bank clerks 2-0 . . . " But then England actually managed a third goal, so we had to change the words of the song slightly.

So the match finished 3-0, and although it wasn't a good game, I still applauded the players despite most others booing the team. Even when my team (Darlo or England) plays shit, it's very rare that I boo them off at the end. I like to get behind the team. Anyway, we were soon out of the ground and onto one of the buses that had been laid on for us to take us back into the city centre. The bus went fucking miles out of the city though, for some reason taking us up the motorway, and took over half an hour to get us to where we were earlier on, which was only about half an hour's walk away from the ground.

Once back in the city centre it was time to drink more beer.

There were shit loads of riot police lined up around the train station area, which is where our hotel was. They were obviously expecting something to go off. We soon found a bar, got the beers in and ordered some food. The menu was in French, but I understood most of it. I tried to be clever when I saw scampi served with something else, then chips separately, so I ordered scampi and chips (in French), expecting the scampi to be in bread crumbs like in England. Got a bit of a shock when the food came though, the scampi was on a separate plate and was complete with all its bits, eyes, claws, tail and everything.

"What the fuck is that?" I said to Mel. I'd never seen scampi in its full glory, didn't realise it would look like that! I ate the chips and then picked at the scampi. It was different I suppose.

We had some more beers in there, and then just as we were about to leave, about half a dozen English lads decided to trash the room they were in to the side, smashing their glasses and knocking the table over. The whole place went silent once they'd gone, and everyone was thinking the same. It was fucking stupid and pointless. There was no locals in there having a go, the staff had been sound with everyone, so why trash a poxy little restaurant? A copper came in a couple of minutes afterwards and spoke to the owner, who seemed a bit stressed out with about 20 English still in there, even if we were being quiet. After that, we went back to the hotel, watched the goings on outside for a bit, which was just people getting pissed, and then crashed out, ready for the drive back the next day.

I felt a bit rough in the morning, but not too bad, and was soon up and eating breakfast, the usual stuff we'd had in France during the summer - bread, coffee and orange juice. After that it was off to catch the bus, which we couldn't find at first. Three others couldn't find the bus and we set off without them, but we found them after a quick drive around the block. The drive back was quite uneventful, and I didn't have much beer knowing that I'd have to drive the car back from Ferrybridge Services that night. Once we got to the ferry, I had a couple of pints, then made Mel shit himself when he was up on deck, looking over the side as we were docking at Dover. I sneaked up to him, slapped him on the shoulder and copied the Blades fan by shouting, "For you zie war ist over . . . !"

The journey back up north seemed to drag, knowing that we had another six or seven hours still to go as we left Dover. One of the Sheffield lot asked the Northampton fans who'd got on at Watford Gap who their main rivals are. The reply was "Peterborough,

Cambridge, Walsall, Barnet . . . all the London teams. We hate everyone really."

I was born just outside Northampton, but left there when I was only a few months old, so it's good to see that they've got a healthy hatred for any other team that could be classed as local.

The rest of the journey was filled with more football talk, crap films on the video, the bus toilet stinking like fuck, and endless cigarettes. After stopping at Watford Gap and Sheffield, we got back to Ferrybridge Services at about 9pm, followed by an hour's drive back to Northallerton. It had been a good couple of days, although not as good as Sweden and the length of the bus journey was a bit of a head banger.

One thing I did notice about Luxemburg was the distinct lack of good looking women. I only counted three, and they were nothing special. Bit of a change from Sweden, that's for sure. Another England trip though, which would surely count in our favour when we came to applying for tickets for the finals of Euro 2000. After all, loyal supporters and all that . . .

England in crisis

(Jamie)

AFTER THE FIRST three matches of the Euro 2000 qualifying group, England had played three, won one (against Luxemburg), drawn one, lost one, scored four, conceded two. Things were not looking good, although being the eternal optimist, I still felt that we'd qualify automatically, we'd just have to win virtually all of our remaining games. Then Glenn Hoddle made a comment during an interview in February, 1999, and we were without a manager.

He holds very strong religious beliefs, which go somewhat beyond the beliefs of most, and basically suggested that disabled people are paying for mistakes that they'd made in previous lives. He's entitled to his opinion, but someone in his position should not be making remarks that will upset and anger millions of people in the country that he serves as national manager. The press had a field day with this one, knowing that they'd finally found the excuse needed to get rid of Hoddle. Maybe he wanted an excuse to leave, so he could follow in the footsteps of David Icke, the former BBC snooker presenter and Coventry goalie who announced that he was Jesus! Everyone's entitled to their beliefs, but when people who are famous for one reason or another make remarks which are out of the norm, they get slated for it. Hoddle should have adopted a more sensitive approach given his job.

Still, if he'd said the same thing a year prior to that, before the World Cup, or if England had won the World Cup, no one would have batted an eyelid. England had done nothing since qualifying for the World Cup, apart from beat Portugal in a friendly, and had only beaten Tunisia and Columbia in the World Cup before going out unluckily to the cheating Argies. After his controversial book and our crap start to the Euro 2000 qualifiers, this was the end of the road for Glenn Hoddle.

This left us with the all too frequent question of who would be the next England manager. Howard Wilkinson, the former Sheffield Wednesday and Leeds United manager who'd taken up a top coaching job at the FA, was installed as caretaker manager for the forthcoming friendly against France at Wembley, which just happened to be on my birthday. I'd always had trouble accepting France as World Champions, and I saw this as our chance to stuff the Frogs and restore some lost pride. I didn't go to the match, but went out in Northallerton and watched it in the pub. It was a shit game though and we lost 2-0. The first time we'd been beaten at home by the French since 1066, and on my birthday as well! Wankers. Fucking humiliating. Still, I got pissed and had a curry, which took my mind off the football and being another year older.

The Football Association were then left with the task of finding Hoddle's replacement. The usual names cropped up in the media - Kevin Keegan, Terry Venables, Bobby Robson, Jack Charlton, Bryan Robson, John Gregory, then people started suggesting a foreign coach such as Alex Ferguson or Gerard Houllier. No fucking chance. They might be good managers for their clubs in England, but managing the English national team is a job for an Englishman. The trouble was though that the more likely candidates were all tied up with their clubs, except Terry Venables and Bobby Robson.

Terry Venables would have been my choice for the job, but he'd left three years earlier after the FA treated him like shit during legal proceedings relating to his alleged dodgy dealings in the past. The FA knew about all that when they appointed him though, and they should have supported him, not shat on him. If a few stuck up officials at the FA could have swallowed their pride and pledged their support for Venables, we'd have a world class manager who had come so close to bringing us success in Euro '96. Look how we'd stuffed Holland 4-1. He'd spent six months preparing for that and we took the piss.

With all his coaching experience and knowledge of the game, he was ideal for the job. The FA wouldn't back down though, and wouldn't appoint a past England manager, which also ruled out my second favourite choice, Bobby Robson. He's done the job before with some degree of success, and had had several years since then managing top clubs abroad. Even though he's getting old, he would have been a sound choice for the short term, and to have someone else with him to groom as a long term successor.

After all the speculation came the announcement that Kevin Keegan, manager of Fulham, would be taking over on a part-time basis for the next four matches, until the FA could find a full-time successor. What bollocks! What's the point of appointing someone to manage the England team on a part-time / temporary basis, when he's already got a full-time job managing a club team? Although potentially the right choice, I doubted Keegan's ability after the way he quit Newcastle United due to the pressure. No manager is under more pressure than the England manager.

He'd had some degree of success at Newcastle and Fulham though, albeit by spending loads of money. I just hoped that he'd sorted his head out since quitting Newcastle, and that the subsequent speculation would be proved correct and he'd be installed as full-time manager, rather than part- time / temporary. No one can doubt his motivational abilities, and he seems to command the respect of his players, something Hoddle was lacking in the end. I just hoped that the press didn't turn on him in the way that they have with other England managers. His first test would be in our next qualifying match against Poland at Wembley.

The Spring of '99

England v Poland

(Matt)

**A FEW WEEKS before this fixture, the England Members Club
(run by the Football Association) had given out details on how
many 'loyalty points' members would get for each match
attended: Home qualifier- one point, away qualifier / friendly -
three points, home friendly - two points.**

When tickets were in demand for the finals in Euro 2000, those
with the most loyalty points would be given priority for tickets. Fair
enough, I thought, until I found out that points only count from the
11th of February, 1999. The bastards. In September, 1998, myself
and a few thousand others had travelled to Sweden for the first
match in this qualifying campaign, and now we find out that our
support would count for nothing when the big game tickets were
handed out. I particularly felt sorry for Jamie and Mel who also
travelled to Luxemburg in October. All those miles, all that money,
and not one loyalty point.

Mind you, come the finals, whose going to get priority for tickets
anyway? An England fan with a high number of loyalty points or a
corporate hospitality wanker who works for the right sponsor? Not a
very hard question to answer .

But anyway, England were at home to Poland and it was a
beautiful sunny day in London. I was going with my mate, Neil,
who's been my best friend for as long as I can remember. Although
he doesn't support anyone in particular, he seems to sympathise
more with the North East teams like Newcastle and Leeds.

The day started in perfect fashion with a Fiorentina pizza (you
know, the one with the fried egg on top), before heading off to
Wembley from Finsbury Park underground in North London. We
made our way straight for the famous Globe pub in Baker Street.
For anyone who doesn't know, it's the main pub for England fans on
match days.

We arrived at Baker Street at around 12.30pm and could not
believe the amount of people in the area. There were St. George's
crosses everywhere. The Globe was so full that we had no chance of
even getting to that side of the street, let alone inside the pub itself.

23

Predictably it was full of nutters singing the usual England songs. Holiday makers on the open top tourist buses driving by were taking photographs. I don't think they knew what to make of it. "Oh my God, look Bob, it's those famous English soccer hooligans," were probably the words of the American tourists.

There was a fair number of police in the area, although there wasn't much sign of trouble. A Polish supporter's bus even drove past The Globe without one bottle being hurled at it! Honestly!

Apart from a few twats doing Nazi salutes, there was a good vibe in the area, although with no chance of getting into a pub there wasn't much point in hanging around. Our best bet was to get a few cans from the off-licence and make our way straight to Wembley.

We had to hide our cans from the police as they wouldn't let anyone with alcohol onto the Underground. Once at Wembley we sat on the grass banks outside the stadium and watched the supporters go by. Couldn't believe how many fans Poland had brought with them. They must have had about 4,000. I wonder how many houses got sold in Poland in order for them to afford the journey!

Inside the stadium there was a good atmosphere with *The Great Escape* being played to warm everyone up. The Poland fans were very vocal, but only seemed to have one song, "Polska! Polska!" It was only a matter of time before the inevitable chant of "If it wasn't for the English you'd be krauts!" was heard from the home support.

As Kevin Keegan led out the team for the first time I was confident we would do the job. He does seem to have the ability to inspire players, and I wasn't disappointed with his appointment. But I was hoping Venables would return as manager. Unfortunately, the FA consider their own personal differences more important than the progress of the national football team. Under Venables if things weren't going well in the first half he seemed to have the ability to turn things around in the second half. Something Hoddle could never do. With him we had our good days and our bad days. And on the bad days he could never turn it around.

Things were all going to plan though as Paul Scholes put us ahead with only nine minutes gone. There were a few Polish fans in our section making their presence felt, so some bloke decided to spit on them and get himself ejected. A bit of a twat really. He waited until the police turned up before he launched it. The small group of Polish fans were harmless, but it's always annoying having away fans in the home section (Manchester United fans please take note) and they were soon moved.

On the pitch things were looking even better as Paul Scholes made it 2-0. It was later claimed that he used his arm to score, but I had a good view of the goal and it seemed like a clean header.

Halfway through the first half I was so desperate for a piss that I had no option but to make a quick run for the toilets. I never do that normally as I'm paranoid about missing a crucial moment in the match. And Sod and his laws being the way they are, Poland went and scored just as my zip was being undone. Typical. Mind you, I'm quite glad I missed it. All I heard was a massive roar from the Poland fans. I've learned my lesson though.

As I returned to my seat, the Polish fans were acting like they'd just won the match, and they'd even invented a second song. Paul Scholes soon saw to them in the second half when he headed home his hat-trick and finished the Poles off. It's possible that he's become the only ginger ever to score a hat-trick at Wembley. Someone check the history books.

Myself and the rest of the people in my section have no memory of what happened on the pitch in the last 15 minutes of the match. On 75 minutes a skinhead spotted something and with outrage shouted, "Oi!". He brought to everyone's attention that one of the stewards had the most ridiculous looking hair in the history of mankind. It was a huge, blonde, over gelled perm in the shape of a modern day cycle helmet. The mockery that came his way was fucking staggering. Nobody cared about what was happening on the pitch, that game was over. All attention was focused on "Wiggy the steward".

His job was to sit on a stool on the dog track, just in front of the first row and monitor the crowd. The poor bastard's job meant he couldn't even turn around. Myself and Neil were fucking pissing ourselves. I was tempted to offer him my sun hat, but it wouldn't have gone a long way to hiding his problem. The songs directed at him were what you would expect from a group of football supporters who were at the scene of a hair crime. "It's a wig!", "What the fucking hell is that?", "Are you Parlour in disguise", "Walking in a Wiggy wonderland", the full works.

To be fair to him he took it all very well, but no opportunity should ever be missed to ridicule a steward. Although this particular steward seemed alright, as are a few others, most of them are little Hitlers who failed their police training course and settled for the next step down.

I'm sick and tired of these illuminous jacket wearing jobsworths telling everyone what to do. I follow Arsenal from the Clock End at

Highbury where they're in your face non-stop. You're faced with the knowledge that if you do anything back to them you're banned from your club for life. They treat fans like scum so any time they get ridiculed by us, it's just a bit of payback. Wiggy the steward gave us all such a good laugh though. I would bet that after the match he went straight to the nearest barber.

The team performed well, and at this stage the thought of not qualifying was not even contemplated. The rest of the day was spent down pubs in the West End. The events of the day, such as the good atmosphere and the sun shining, brought back memories of last year's World Cup in France. It made me even more desperate to see us qualify for the European Championships. Euro 2000 will be a great event and England must be there. Plus I fancy a holiday in Belgium and Holland. Altogether now, "Kevin Keegan's blue and white army!"

England v Sweden

(Jamie)

After our win over Poland in March we were quite confident about the Sweden game, despite the slightly disappointing draw in Hungary in a friendly match. I didn't bother going to that, as me, Matt and Darren (another Darlo fan from Northallerton), were booked on a week long coach trip to Bulgaria, which would set off on the night after the Sweden game, stop off in Budapest, stay in Sofia for the Bulgaria match, then stop off in Vienna for a night on the way back. But, due to the war in Kosovo, changing venues and lack of interest in the trip, the tour operator (who we went to Luxemburg and later Poland with) cancelled it. What a fucker! It would have been a killer of a journey, but we were all looking forward to that one.

They did offer to find cheap flights and accommodation for us at one of the coastal resorts, but by the time they offered that the three of us had all cancelled our leave from work and made other arrangements. We'd just have to make do with Poland in September.

So, what would have been the start of a week long holiday taking in two England matches was just a weekend in London for the Sweden match at Wembley. On the train there was me (Darlo), Darren (Darlo), Mel (Darlo), Adrian (Darlo), Shaun (Man Utd) and Al

(Liverpool), all from Northallerton, and we'd be meeting Matt (Arsenal) at Kings Cross. Me and Daz would be stopping at Matt's, Shaun and Al would be stopping in a hotel in central London, and Mel and Adrian were catching the 7pm train back home.

Once down there, Shaun and Al headed off to find their hotel down the West End, leaving the rest of us to go to The Globe on Baker Street, where everyone changes tube trains on the way to Wembley. We got there at 10.55am, and there was about 100 people queuing up behind crush barriers, waiting to get in! What a sight. At 11am, everyone piled in, I went to the bar and waited for about ten minutes before getting served. It's a great pub though on England match days, and after standing outside in the sun for a bit, we all headed downstairs where there was a fair bit of room. The beers were flowing and the place filled up with others coming in from outside, and then the singing started.

It was a great laugh in there, with one song going on non-stop for about ten minutes. "When I was young, I had no sense, so I bought a flute, for fifty pence, but the only tune, that I could play, was the fuck the pope, and the IRA . . . Na-na na na, na-na na na, na na na na-na, na-na na na . . . When I was young, I had no sense . . . "

There was also the usual England songs, and after a few more beers we went back outside to enjoy our last pint in the sun. Loads of tourist buses were going past, with loads of Japs, Yanks and whatever looking on in bemusement, frantically reaching for their camcorders. I just couldn't resist starting several renditions of *No Surrender* for the tourists!

It was soon time to head off to the match so we got the tube up to Wembley, which took about half an hour. Once there we slowly walked up Wembley Way, then got round to the part of the stadium we were in. Me, Daz, Matt and Adrian were at one end, Mel, Shaun and Al were down at the other end. We were sat right down at the front in the second row, about ten feet away from the family enclosure, so we knew right away that the atmosphere wouldn't be too good. The teams soon came out, and it was time for us to beat Sweden and take control of the qualifying group.

After a passionately sung national anthem, the match got underway with a few promising signs early on. It soon died down though and became a crap game, with England hardly creating any chances at all, and Sweden looking content for the draw which would leave them in command of the group. The atmosphere was lacking, apart from the singing of *The Great Escape*, and the passion from the England players was certainly lacking. It was such an unmemorable match.

Half-time came and went, during which time I saw Baggy (Darlo fan from Keighley, West Yorkshire, but now living in Newton Aycliffe, County Durham) who was flying out to Bulgaria the next day for the England match four days later. The second half was not much better than the first, and things became worse when Paul Scholes got sent off for a reckless tackle. So again, just like over in Stockholm, we were down to ten men and looking desperate. A few chances were created later on, but despite the players putting in a bit of extra effort towards the end, the match finished 0-0 which virtually ensured that Sweden would finish top of the group, leaving us to fight for the play-off position. At least I managed to shout loads of abuse at Henrik Larsson every time he was nearby - "Larsson, you Fenian scum!"

When we left Wembley Stadium, I tried my hardest to wind up a couple of Swedes who were walking in front of us. As we were all shuffling along I was constantly kicking the heels of the Swede in front of me, but got no response. So Daz kicks him in the leg, the Swede looks around at me, and turns away again. Bottled it! Wankers, coming over here and getting a point out of the match!

By the time we met up with Mel, Shaun and Al, it was pissing down with rain. To avoid the crowds, Matt took us away from the main concourse and away from Wembley, and down another street off to the side. For some reason (England not winning perhaps?) I was pissed off to fuck. Then I notice three lads wearing white shirts walking in the opposite direction. Nothing unusual, but as they get closer and then passed us, I realised the shirts carried the badge of the scum. Monkey hangers from Hartlepool wearing the away shirt (they're called monkey hangers because the people of Hartlepool hung a monkey during the Napoleonic wars, having fiest accused it of being a French spy!). So, without wanting to do anything out of order (there were seven of us, three of them, amongst hundreds of people and probably on camera), me and Daz tried provoking them for a reaction by shouting "monkey-hangers", "chimp-chokers", before Daz starts singing "Darl-ing-ton, Darl-ing-ton, Darl-ing-ton!"

We got no reaction though, it was pissing down, and we needed beer, so we carried on and finally got to the tube station.

Everyone on the tube was quiet, wet, and gutted that we hadn't beaten Sweden. The journey back to Kings Cross seemed to last forever. Once there Shaun and Al went off to their hotel down the West End, and the rest of us went to the Flying Scotsman pub just around the corner, a small pub with strippers where all football fans seem to stop off after watching their club or the England team play in London. It was good to see something decent after the shit match we'd just seen.

Mel and Adrian left at 7pm to get the train back up north, leaving me, Matt, and Daz, to head off down to the West End in search of some good pubs. Mel said later that there was a pissed up Jock doing everyone's heads in on the train, saying that he was off to the Czech Republic to watch Scotland, but was going back home for his passport! He fell asleep later on so Mel nicked one of his shoes that he'd taken off and left it on Northallerton station! So he was probably hopping around Glasgow Central shouting, "Hey you, where's my shoe, by the way!"

Me, Matt and Daz got the tube down to Trafalgar Square and wandered around looking for pubs. In the first pub we waited at the bar for five minutes, only to be told by some snobby cow of a barmaid that "football colours are not allowed". What a fucking piss take! I was wearing a navy blue polo shirt which had the England three lions badge on, and they didn't serve me for that. There were people in there with purple hair and scruffy clothes, but they served them. But, rather than argue, we went off to find somewhere else.

The next two pubs were the same, until we found a small place near Trafalgar Square that seemed full of locals. Not a bad place to have a couple of pints, but not too lively either. After that, we headed up towards Soho. The place is full of all sorts of poncey, poofy bars, no decent traditional English pubs.

We finally found a pub that looked okay, went in, asked for a pint, and the geek behind the bar says, "Sorry, no football colours."

So I said, "This is a smart t-shirt with a badge on that represents this country, how is that a problem?"

He just said, "Sorry, it's the rules."

So I replied, "Fuck off, you poof!"

Bunch of fucking wankers! What's this country coming to when you can't walk into a pub in the capital of England, wearing a t-shirt with an England badge on it?! Yet at the same time, they allow people to wear all sorts of scruffy, poncey, poofy shit and serve them no problem. London's pubs have become shit, too continental and poncey. The only real pubs are in the suburbs. The Globe at Baker Street being the obvious exception that springs to mind.

Anyway, enough of slagging off the West End. We finally found a pub that would tolerate someone wearing "football colours", and had a few pints in there. We went to a few more pubs later on, and ended up getting quite pissed and having a good laugh. The night was finished off with a Chinese take away from Crouch End, where Matt lives, before crashing out.

On the Sunday we got the bus down to Kings Cross, spent four hours in the Duke Of York pub, got pissed, and then got the train home, having met up with Shaun and Al at the station. It had been a good weekend, it was just a shame that England didn't win and we weren't going over to Bulgaria.

I sat and watched the Bulgaria match at home, feeling left out because I wasn't there. England started off well enough, with Alan Shearer scoring to put us 1-0 up, but Bulgaria soon got back into it and equalised. There were a few chances created, and Jonathan Woodgate of Leeds had another good game after making his debut against Hungary, but the performance as a whole was lacking and the match ended 1-1. Bollocks! That meant we had to beat Luxemburg and Poland in our last two games just to qualify for the play-offs.

The optimism from a week earlier had turned to desperation in the space of five days. Despite the result, after speaking to Baggy and one of Daz's mates from Thirsk, it sounded as though everyone had a good time over there, with cheap beer and hot weather. At least we had Poland to look forward to, albeit with a sense of nervousness. Not really because of the prospect of getting done over by a load of Poles, but because of the need to win the game or be virtually out of Euro 2000 (a draw would mean Poland would need just a point against Sweden in October).

The Autumn of '99

England v Luxemburg

(Matt)

DURING THE SUMMER break when there's no football, I had taken the time to attend a match in the Cricket World Cup. India v Australia at the Oval. Although the Aussies won, it was quite a refreshing experience, and the one thing I noticed more than anything in comparison to football, was the amount of respect you get shown as a spectator. The authorities at cricket grounds actually treat fans like paying customers! Plus, you can't knock a sport that lets you drink pints inside the stadium.

Even the stewards were relaxed. One bloke ran onto the pitch after a four was scored and started waving a flag about. The stewards took immediate action and told him to stop messing about and that he should return to his seat! Hang on a second, if he did that at a football match, he'd be arrested, banned for life, and prosecuted. The announcer even made a plea for fans to show some respect and avoid the crease when they invaded the pitch at the end of the match!

Earlier in the year I was at Villa Park for the Arsenal v Man Utd FA Cup semi-final replay. Upon the final whistle a few hundred Man Utd fans ran onto the pitch in a spontaneous celebration of what had been a great advertisement for English football. The next day it was called a disgrace and questions were asked about how it was allowed to happen. Although the sight of all those Man U fans running around the pitch made me wish I had a bow and arrow, it was a natural reaction on their part and it's what football's all about. And the sooner the authorities realise it the better.

But anyway the Cricket World Cup was over, and it was back to the number one sport in the world. The Gooners had a slightly shaky start to the season, so the international break came as a welcome respite from domestic football. Our chances of qualifying for the 2000 finals were seriously dented by draws against Sweden and Bulgaria. If we failed to beat Poland in our last match then we stood little chance of qualifying. But first we had to beat Luxemburg at home.

Being the pessimist that I am, I said before the game that I would settle for 2-0. Even though it was Luxemburg, all I cared about was getting the three points that would set us up for Poland. I was going to Wembley with an old school friend called Neil (not the same Neil from the Poland game). Neil's roots are Jamaican which he respects, but he was born and bred in England and therefore considers himself an Englishman. And rightly so. Although he's a good mate of mine, he's a Spurs fan which means that when talking about football he's liable to come out with some complete and utter shit.

I know my opinion's biased, but Spurs fans talk more crap than any other fans in the country. An arsehole head count at White Hart Lane on match day would be in the region of 35,000. To prove my point, I've even heard Spurs fans on radio phone-ins saying that Justin Edinburgh deserves an England call up. And they're serious as well. I mean for fuck's sake, that guy wouldn't even have got an England call up during World War Two.

While on the subject of scum, the press were carrying on with their usual ways. The stick they handed out to Alan Shearer was well over the top. Alright, the guy's got an attitude problem, but in terms of converting chances he's still our most clinical striker. The reason he's not been scoring is because he plays for a poor Newcastle team who don't create the chances.

I remember two weeks before Euro 96, Shearer was going though a similar problem. The *Daily Mirror*'s back page headline at the time was "The worst striker in Europe". Well a few weeks later guess who changed their tune and jumped on the Shearer bandwagon?

But anyway, myself and Neil had left it late to get to Wembley. It was 2pm and we were still in Finsbury Park in North London. An hour seems like enough time to get there, but the London Underground can never be trusted. Because of national anthems it always seems more important to get to the ground on time for internationals than it does domestic matches. Neil assured me that the quickest way to get there was by over ground train to Wembley Central. Being a Yid, I'm surprised that he even knew where Wembley was. He was right though. From Marylebone in central London we got to Wembley Central in under ten minutes. All those years I've been taking the Underground's slow Metropolitan line, when a better service has been available.

It was a full house at Wembley, although I couldn't see any Luxemburg fans in the stadium. Within minutes of the game kicking off it was clear that we were going to walk all over them. Shearer set things off with a penalty, and then made it 2-0 with a beautiful finish from 20 yards. Take that you tabloid scum! For the third goal, Kieron Dyer ran into the box and was fouled. The Luxemburg players stopped as they saw the referee put his whistle to his mouth. The referee then changed his mind as Dyer passed to MacManaman to make it 3-0 with a simple tap in. The Luxemburg players looked pissed off at the ref, and you can understand why. By half-time it was 5-0.

The best thing we could do would be to take it easy in the second half, and save all the energy for the Poles. After all, goal difference would not play a part in this group whatever happened in the remaining games. If England and Poland finish level on points then it would come down to how the two teams fared against each other in the two group games.

And save our energy we did, as the second half was a non event. Predictably when the game turns into an anti-climax the Mexican Wave decided to appear. One thing I've noticed, particularly at England games, is that some people get really offended by the Mexican Wave. The bloke in front of us took real exception to it. When everyone was sat down he stood up, and as the Mexican Wave came our way he made his point by sitting down and calling everyone wankers. I don't really care either way. To be fair the Mexican Wave can look good, but then again it does represent the fact that there's fuck all happening on the pitch.

Michael Owen made everyone happy in the last minute with the best goal of the match from 25 yards. 6-0, you can't really ask for more than that. These games are always no-win situations. No matter what we do, the critics (and especially Mark Lawrenson) will always say how poor the opposition were. Remember Poland could only beat this lot 3-2.

The train journey back to Marylebone was spent arguing over North London differences. I was making the valid point that Spurs fans steal all Arsenals songs, while Neil was talking some rubbish about how 'George' is gonna sort them out this season. Oh, it's George these days is it? One minute it's 'Scum', next minute it's 'the man in the overcoat', and now after winning one Mickey Mouse trophy it's 'George'! Pathetic.

Marylebone Station is only two minutes away from Baker Street so we thought we'd try our luck and see if we could get into The Globe. But when we got there we were surprised to see that it was shut. Maybe the police closed it, fearing there might be trouble.

The evening was spent down a snooker club in North London. All

I could think about was travelling to Poland for the game on Wednesday night. It would be my first away trip with England since the defeat in Stockholm last September. We were supposed to travel to Bulgaria by coach in the summer, but the war in Yugoslavia messed up our travel plans. Selfish bastards! Sofia is only 50 miles from the border of Yugoslavia, and I don't think that the people of that region would have taken too kindly to seeing a coach passing by that had Union Jacks hanging from the windows.

England fans seem to attract trouble wherever they go and I had to laugh at the thought of it kicking off with the Serbian army. You'd get all these Man City fans coming back home saying, "We fucking took Yugoslavia, nobody's ever taken Yugoslavia before. The fucking Serbs bottled it."

That's a thought, why did we waste all that money bombing Yugoslavia? They should have just hired England's travelling support in Bulgaria to steam into the Serbs on their way back home. Mind you if they did they'd still get the blame by the media. "English yobs attack Nazi ethnic cleansers in shameful scenes in Serbia." "Why do we tolerate these thugs?"

But anyway, Luxemburg had been seen to and confidence should be high after an easy victory. All attention would now be on the match with Poland which is a must win. See you in Warsaw.

Poland v England

(Matt)

WHENEVER I'VE WATCHED English sides play on the TV in countries like Poland, Moldova, the Ukraine, etc., I've always thought to myself, "What kind of madman follows them over there?"

How can anyone travel to those parts of the world just to watch a football match? Well, after paying £107 to the travel company, Northern Holidays, I was to become one of those people.

My previous trips with England, the 1998 World Cup in France and the Euro 2000 qualifier in Stockholm were both great experiences, but Poland sounded a lot harsher. Plus this time Jamie, Mel, Daz and me would be travelling all the way to Poland by coach.

Our attitude would be the same as it was for our previous England trips. We were going for a laugh and to enjoy the experience. We would not be looking for trouble, but if trouble were to find us then we would not be afraid to defend ourselves.

I'd already suffered earlier in the day at the hands of Jamie's now ex-fiancee. She decided to try out her recently acquired self-defence techniques on me while down the pub. It hurt like fuck as Jamie just looked on and laughed.

The tickets we had for the match were hard to come by as England were only allocated 1,900 tickets. The price of the ticket was £36. This came as an unwelcome surprise given the then exchange rate of 1.6 Zlotys to the pound. £36 was not a black market price, it was the price set by the Polish FA. Surely you could buy a house in Poland for that price? As usual, when it comes to ripping people off, it's open season on English football supporters.

The coach was to depart from Ferrybridge Services (near Leeds) at 4.30 am Tuesday, and arrive in Warsaw at 11:30 am Wednesday. I didn't think they were giving themselves much time to get there, but I gave them the benefit of the doubt as I was sure that they must have known what they were doing. Jamie was driving down to Ferrybridge, and after picking up Mel and Daz, we were ready to begin our journey.

It was three 'o' clock in the morning, and the roads were nice and clear as we made our way from Northallerton to Ferrybridge in Jamie's Ford Fiesta. The car resembled the cockpit of a spitfire as we listened to themes from films like *633 Squadron*, *Dambusters*, *The Longest Day*, and *The Great Escape,* along with a few England football songs like *World In Motion*. Just what we needed to raise the spirits for the start of what was going to be a long journey.

Once at Ferrybridge, we saw a coach pull up with the words 'Pat's Coaches - North Wales' written on the back of it. "That can't be our coach," we said to each other. "Can't get taken on an England trip by a bunch of Taffs!"

But sure enough, it was. To be honest, I couldn't care less if they were from Outer Mongolia, so long as they were to get us to Warsaw on time. At first they seemed all right, although the main rep looked like a cross between Droopy The Dog and Mark Lawrenson. Looking like Droopy The Dog is bad enough, but Mark Lawrenson, that's just taking the piss. As we were the first to be picked up, and the only fans to be picked up at Ferrybridge, it meant we were able to take the seats at the back of the coach which I was delighted about. We would later come to regret it.

We then departed to Hull to pick up the rest of the coach load. After passing the attractive Humber Bridge we arrived in Hull and were joined by another 40 or 50 people. They were all big lads, some of them quite hard looking, and to be honest I wasn't complaining. Poland sounded like it could be quite dangerous, and if we were to get caught up in any trouble we would be in good company.

Apart from a few Doncaster fans, they were all Hull City. Although all friends, there seemed to be a rivalry between those from West Hull and those from East Hull, with each one thinking the other side of the city was crap.

After we had each paid £20 bond money in case of damages, the coach full of Hull City, Doncaster, Darlington, and one Gooner, was finally ready to go to Poland.

The loudest bunch of Hull City fans were sat just in front of us and spent the journey to Dover ribbing each other at every opportunity. Particularly one lad who got it bad when it was discovered that the pillow he had brought with him had a nice flowery pattern on it.

After five hours of the journey I was disturbed to find out that we were only at Lakeside Services in Essex. It was there that we would meet up with a second coach load from Northern Holidays coming via the North West, and mainly full of Manchester City and Oldham fans. They would follow us on our journey.

By the time we arrived in Dover we were already two hours behind schedule. There seemed to be no urgency from the drivers to get there in time, which annoyed me as it meant less time to look around the centre of Warsaw. Being two hours late was helped by the fact we stopped off at service stations for a total of one and a half hours. The reason at the time - "We're ahead of schedule, lads." Incompetent Welsh twats.

While on the ferry, myself and Mel went up to the top deck with a couple of pints and watched the white cliffs fade away into the distance, reminiscing about the time we'd had in France the year before during the World Cup. Once in French waters, we were able to throw our empties into the sea and then join the others down below as we arrived in Calais.

After stocking up on beer in a cash and carry, we were out of France and through Belgium within about five hours. By the time we crossed the German border, light was fading and alcohol levels were rising. The coach was becoming full of life, with everyone on their feet and singing, "Two World Wars and one World Cup, we won!", followed by the whole coach with their arms outstretched like the wings of an airplane, singing the theme from *Dambusters*. It must have been a sight for other drivers on the motorway.

This must have gone on for about an hour before we were pulled over by the police. It quietened everyone down, as all we wanted to do was show the police that we were all nice quiet lads who just wanted to carry on with our journey. Mind you, 50 pissed up England fans singing on a coach can hardly be described as disturbing the peace. Well, from the point of view that we weren't harming anyone on the outside. They soon let us go and we were on our way.

The drivers had decided that we would stop off in the city of Dortmund for about an hour. Not a bad idea. Having had the chance to see Dortmund, it looked like the kind of city that has had to build itself up after being destroyed in the war. For a modern city it was quite a nice place to be. Nice bars, nice vibes, etc.

We recognised one of the Man City lads from the other coach as being one of those arrested on the train back from Lyon after we'd been knocked out of the World Cup. Up to a hundred riot police and security guards boarded the train because a few people didn't have tickets, so we talked about that and other things with him for a bit.

Although we were only there for just over an hour, it was enough time for some of the Hull City lads to pick a fight with some local Turks. It resulted in two of them being arrested. One of them was let free after reading negative on a breath test. God only knows how, as he'd been drinking all day. The other was being held by the police and it turned out that the only way for him to be released was for a £300 bail to be paid. It meant that we all had to pay £5 each out of our bond money to get him out.

I wasn't too happy about that. I was hoping to get the full £20 bond money back at the end of the trip, but I suppose that we couldn't just leave him there. After waiting an hour on the coach for it to be sorted out he was finally let go and ready to join us. Before he boarded, someone shouted out, "Oi lads, thunderous applause when he gets on."

I thought to myself, "Hang on a second. He's just cost us all a fiver each, and held up our journey by an hour, and you want us to give him a hero's return?"

We were soon back on the road and on our way to Poland. It had been a long day and it was time to get some much needed sleep. I was hoping that by the time I woke up in the morning we would be arriving in Poland, but come 7.00am, we were still a good three hours from the Polish border.

As expected it had been difficult trying to get some sleep on the coach. And anyone who's never tried to take a piss in a coach toilet has never experienced hardship in their lives. It turns out that since we left Dortmund, the German police had insisted that we had a police escort out of their country so that we wouldn't cause any more trouble. Great, so now it's not up to us where we stop and how fast we go. Mind you the way the Welsh were driving we couldn't go much slower.

Once over the Polish border we stopped at a service station for about an hour. I don't think most people realised how far away Warsaw was from the Germany - Poland border. They seemed shocked when they found out we had another 300 miles to travel. I wondered why I seemed to be the only one who was pissed off about all the delays we'd experienced.

The drive from then on was one of the most frustrating journeys I've ever had. The driver must have only been doing about 40-50 miles per hour. It was clear that it was a ploy to get us there late so that there would be no chance of us getting into trouble. This made my blood boil as I was desperate to see the centre of Warsaw. I felt like going into a violent rage by storming down the aisle and stamping on the driver's head, then landing a punch on his mate, Droopy, but that wouldn't get us to Warsaw any quicker.

To make matters worse, the video they were showing on the coach was Roy 'Chubby' Brown's own feature film, *UFO*. Possibly the most tedious man on this planet. The only comedy being the fact that he honestly believes himself to be controversial. No Roy, you're just a sad old man.

The final icing on the cake was that we were seated at the back. Now I said before that we would regret sitting at the back of the coach. With the toilet being right next to us, and the number of trips being made to it particularly high due to the amount of beer that had been drunk, the aroma of piss started to creep though the door and made life a living hell for everyone within sniffing distance.

When we arrived on the outskirts of Warsaw at around 6.30pm, we were pulled over by the police and had our passports checked. Once we were able to set off we were pulled over again within about five minutes. We all just sat on the coach while the drivers talked to the police. You could see that everyone on the outside was staring at us like we were animals in a cage. After a while the general response just couldn't help being, "Who the fuck are you looking at?"

After 20 minutes of waiting, frustrations were beginning to grow. We'd done nothing wrong to provoke all this police presence. After all, it was the Polish fans who had spent the last two days ambushing England fans. And we were getting sick of being stared at like we were on board an alien ship that had just landed. Our country fought a war for them and this is how they treat us.

A man from the other coach then came on to explain what was happening. He had done the same the night before when the Hull City fan was in German custody. It became obvious to us that he was some kind of undercover police intelligence officer who was sent out to monitor us. He was not with Northern Holidays and yet was forever in contact with the police. He also travelled by himself which is not the sort of thing you do when watching football abroad. Plus the fact that despite being a Spurs fan, he didn't seem like the kind of guy who would find it difficult to make friends.

To cover himself, he kept on saying, "I'm just a normal football fan just like you, I just wanna see the game." Which was probably true, but he was still an undercover copper.

He explained to us that earlier on there had been 50 Polish youths waiting for us outside our hotel with basketballs! BASKETBALLS?! Fucking hell, no wonder we had to fight a war for this lot. Is that what they used against Hitler's tanks?

He quickly realised his mistake and informed us that it was in fact baseball bats that they were carrying. Apparently, they had been waiting there for us at around midday, the time when we were supposed to check in. Unfortunately they didn't bank on the fact that we were travelling with Pat's Coaches.

Once we arrived at the hotel there was only enough time for us to check in and then get taken to the stadium by the coach. The drivers then had the cheek to charge us all £4.00 each for them to take us to the stadium and back. The reason? They were working beyond their hours. Hardly our fucking fault. Why should we reward them for their own incompetence?

Everyone was so desperate to get to the stadium that they eventually paid up, even although transportation to and from the ground was part of the package we paid for. The cheeky bastards.

Once at the stadium it turns out that a few of the Hull City lads didn't have tickets for the match. They were planning on taking their chances and would try to casually walk in with the rest of the crowd, like what happened in Rome two years before when the police feared crowd congestion. On this occasion there were people at the gate checking for tickets, but the perimeter fence going round the entrance was not well guarded, and was in the form of the front of a prison cell. So once everyone with tickets entered the stadium, they just passed their ticket stubs to the people outside. Simple as that.

Just before kick-off, I was beginning to feel the nerves. I was worried that we'd used up all our luck against Poland in recent years. These games are never high scoring and I could only see a score of 0-0, 1-1, or 1-0 either way. There had been talk beforehand about the intimidating atmosphere of this particular stadium, but to be honest it wasn't that bad. I'm sure every member of the England team has experienced a lot worse than that.

We didn't start playing until 20 minutes into the match, and from then on up to half-time we were unlucky not to be at least a goal up. About ten minutes into the second half, a flare was fired into the England enclosure. It hit a lad in the stomach who, like the rest of us, was too busy watching the match to avoid it. I don't think he was too hurt, but it must have been a shock.

The Polish fans then sent off two more well-aimed flares into our section along with rocks. The rocks were only the size of an apple, but at the speed and distance they were coming from, if one were to hit someone in the head it could have killed him. This sparked an angry reaction from the England fans who moved with venom towards the Polish. I thought there was no way they could get to them as there was a 15 foot high steel fence to get through, plus some barbed wire. The Polish fans were in a section about ten yards away from this fence that segregated both sets of fans.

After the Poles sent off two more flares towards us, one of which hit another lad who wasn't looking, the provocation was complete. The ferocity of the England fans response made me realise why we're so good at winning wars. They managed to tear down the fence, rip up seats, and throw them at the Poles, who also threw what they could back.

You could see the headlines before they'd been written. "England's night of shame." "England fans go on rampage." "Why do we tolerate these thugs?" I wasn't proud of the response, but I wasn't ashamed either. The Polish police never bothered to protect us, and were happy to let their fans get away with what they could. After the England fans gave a bit back we never had any more trouble from the Polish fans. But as usual, despite what their own fans had got away with, the riot police came down hard on the English, and only the English. Same old story.

Back to the match, and it was getting a little desperate. It got to that stage where you just knew that we weren't going to score. We didn't seem to create any clear cut chances, and as the final whistle went neither set of supporters was too happy, although the result put the Poles in a far stronger position than us. I think the Polish supporters felt that they were going to beat us, guaranteeing them a place in the play-offs.

We were kept behind in the stadium for an hour after the game. The atmosphere was very morbid and quiet. Most people just sitting down and contemplating the fact that our Euro 2000 dream looked over before it had even really began. Kevin Keegan walked passed us a couple of times to do interviews. He was surrounded by a ton of security, and received generous applause from the fans in our section, which he seemed to appreciate. The only other thing to liven things up was the appearance of sports journalist, Rob Shepherd, by the players tunnel. He received a barrage of abuse before slithering away down it into the bowels of the stadium.

The journey from the ground back to the hotel was trouble free. We were advised to go back to the hotel as it was considered too dodgy to go into town as apparently gangs of Poles were picking off small groups of English. As keen as I was to see the centre of Warsaw, I'd rather not end the evening by being stabbed. The hotel was massive and not bad for a two star. Our room was near the top floor, and had a balcony with a view of the Warsaw suburbs. I can't speak for the centre of the city, but the rest of it was bleak. Even earlier in the day when the sun was shining, it was still bleak. No prospect. You could tell that the whole of the city must have been destroyed during the war as all the buildings were modern. At least the women were nice.

Before we crashed out, we had a few beers on the balcony and discussed future England trips, and who we'd like to get drawn against in the World Cup qualifiers, seeing as Euro 2000 seemed like a distant dream. "Denmark would be nice, we've never been to Switzerland, Spain would be great . . . Nah, you'd get all those arseholes from Ibiza coming to join us . . . "

As we were stood outside the hotel the next morning waiting to board the coach, it turned out that another £5 of our bond money had gone. Apparently the night before, a few of the Hull City lads had caused some damage to the hotel. They couldn't get in what they thought was their hotel room, so they thought it would be a good idea to kick the door down - much to the surprise of the couple who were in bed at the time. Another door was also kicked in, a window smashed, and a bar of soap damaged! I quite liked the Hull City lads, but would like them more if they didn't keep costing me money.

The drive from Warsaw to the German border was with a police escort. On approaching the German border, we kept on passing these rough looking prostitutes on a road near some woods. There were a lot of truckers on the road who must have been their main bait.

At the service station by the border, I was disgusted to see one of the lads from the other coach wearing a Spurs shirt. The rational side of me thought, "We're all out here supporting England, club loyalties don't matter, this is England United." But the true side of me thought, "Get that piece of filth that you call a shirt off your back, and get back on the coach and hang your head in shame, you dirty Spurs scum." I know that sounds harsh, but Arsenal and Spurs just don't get on.

To cross the border, the Germans had the cheek to charge us £100. I notice they didn't charge us to leave. Once again they wouldn't let us through their country without a police escort, which meant that we couldn't stop anywhere unless the police felt like it. Meanwhile, the Hull City lads had worked out that with £10 bond money still left, it was enough for two more arrests, or one more arrest and one act of vandalism.

When we did stop off at a service station, being forced in there by about a hundred police, I said to one plain clothed officer, "We've done nothing wrong, you're treating us like prisoners," to which he replied, "We're worried about you". Bollocks! All this police presence must have been costing the German taxpayer. So there you go, every cloud has a silver lining.

It was 10.00 pm and my hard-drinking cousin, Jamie, was falling asleep. He looked drained. "What's wrong with you?" I asked.

"I'm knackered."

After years of being called a soft Southern bastard for not always keeping up with the pace, the words, "You soft Northern bastard" felt particularly sweet. After watching a couple more films, it was time to try and get some sleep myself.

By the time I woke up we were still in Germany. I was preparing myself for the smug comments from people back home. "You went all that way just to see a 0-0 draw, was it really worth it?"

I hate it when people come out with crap like that. As if when we booked the package the 0-0 draw was included. We didn't know what the score was going to be. The problem was that if someone were to say something like that to me it would have touched a real nerve. Those sort of comments didn't matter when we came home from the World Cup and the defeat in Stockholm. Both those trips were about more than just football. Even though the results on the pitch went wrong we had some consolation from the time we had off it. But on this occasion it turned out that we had travelled all that way just to watch 90 minutes of football. As passionate about the game as we are, we couldn't help but feel a little disappointed.

After finally seeing the last of the police at the Belgium border, the trip from then on to Dover was mostly uneventful. Once again, due to Welsh incompetence, we missed at least two more ferries so by the time we arrived back in England we were already almost five hours behind schedule. Whilst on the M25 on the outskirts of south east London, Droopy and his drivers heard that there had been an accident on the M25 causing delays. They then made the bizarre decision to cut through London, get on the North Circular, and take the M1 up north. Now London's bad at the best of times, but bear in mind that it was 5pm on a Friday. You don't just cut through London like it's some sort of small village.

Living in London, you'd think I'd be happy about this detour, but I couldn't get out as I had left my keys up at Jamie's house, expecting to arrive at Ferrybridge in the afternoon, then have a night out in Northallerton. I had a coach booked early Saturday morning for London in time to get me back for the Arsenal v Aston Villa match at Highbury. I needed my keys for the weekend, so I had no option but to stay on the coach. To add insult we wouldn't even get back to Northallerton before closing time.

I thought that if Droopy was not a complete idiot, he would change his mind and continue on the M25. But the moron went and tried his luck through London. After two hours we were still only in south west London. I was beginning to wish that we had been taken to Poland by those Outer Mongolians. In fact an Outer Mongolian with no hearing, only 10% sight, and one leg, would have done a better job than these thick Taffs. A chant from the back of the coach of "Sheep, sheep, sheepshaggers!" was the least they deserved.

Daz and Mel were so frustrated that they picked up their bags, got off at Earls Court, and made their way to Kings Cross to take the train back to Northallerton. I hope it sent a message to Droopy that his coach service was crap. Myself and Jamie were tempted to join them, but didn't have the £40 train fare to throw away, plus the fact that the car was at Ferrybridge Services anyway. We finally arrived back at Ferrybridge at 11.30 pm, nine hours off schedule.

The trip had its good moments, but I would not advise anyone to travel abroad by coach to watch football. You're not in control of what you do, you don't see much of the city you're visiting, and worst of all, you're in the hands of the police who will treat you like prisoners being transferred from one prison to another. In future I would only travel by planes and trains. Then I remembered. I'd got a coach from Darlington to London first thing in the morning. Shit. Oh well, it's pretty much all over for England now, I'll just have to rely on the Gooners to cheer me up. Come on you Reds!

(Jamie)

THE MONTH BETWEEN our 0-0 draw in Poland and the game between Sweden and Poland seemed to last forever. Now that England had played all eight qualifying matches and were in second place, on level points with Poland but ahead having beaten them at Wembley, it all boiled down to this . . .

- if Poland won or drew, we were out, but if they lost, we were through to the play-offs. Normally, I'd expect Sweden to win easily against Poland in Stockholm. They're a much better team, playing at home, and they'd had a good qualifying campaign. The thing was, they'd already qualified in top spot and had nothing to play for other than pride, whereas Poland would be going all out for the all important point. Added to that was the usual paranoia that no one likes us and would not be doing us any favours.

In the build up to the match, the Swedish players were saying that they'd do their best to win, some saying they'd be helping England (the English club based players), others saying that they'd be doing it for pride and to boost their place in the FIFA rankings. The Poles meanwhile became confident and gobby, saying how shit England had become, and after our qualifying campaign, it was difficult to disagree. It's a sad state of affairs when the future of the English national team for the next year depends on the outcome of a match we're not even competing in.

When the big day came, I woke up thinking, "This is it. Judgement day!" And England weren't even playing. I didn't watch the match as I had the fun task of looking at houses with my fiancee of the time (but no more), during which time I got a phone call on my mobile from Dan, my brother who lives in Norway, to say that Sweden were 1-0 up. Fucking yes! Come on Sweden! After another house visit and a trip to the supermarket, I got another call to say that it was 2-0 and the match was over! I was so fucking happy! England had done it. We'd qualified for the play-offs! Cheers Sweden (even Larsson scored, which seemed a bit ironic). So that was it. Part one of England's Great Escape was completed.

England v Belgium

(Jamie)

AFTER THE RELIEF of Sweden beating Poland on the Saturday to ensure that England finished second in the group, we had a friendly match against Belgium to go to at the Stadium Of Light in Sunderland.

Belgium are definitely the weakest of the co-hosts of Euro 2000, and they'd been crap when I saw them at the World Cup in France. This would be a nice easy match in a stadium that I'd never been to, and the chance for a good day's drinking. Four of us went up to Sunderland on the train - me, Daz, Adrian and Shaun. After an hour's journey up to Newcastle, we changed trains and were on our way to Sunderland, this train being much more packed than the last one.

I got talking to a couple of Donny Rovers lads on the train, who I know from years ago when a mate of mine from college who was a big Donny fan took me around Doncaster for a night on the piss. I'd been down there several times and always had a good laugh with them all, especially when hearing tales about their exploits following England away. It was about three or four years since I last saw them so it was good to see them again, even if my mate from college, Simon (or Cookie to those from Donny) wasn't there as he now lives in Tenerife with his girlfriend.

Anyway, we were soon in Sunderland and in search of beer. There were loads of coppers around, obviously wary of rumours that Newcastle were bringing a mob down to take on the Sunderland mob. We soon found a decent pub and had a few beers in there, along with a mixture of others but mainly Mackems.

After a while we headed off towards the stadium, stopping at a pub on the way called the City Tavern. It was full of Sunderland fans with a few others about, but it was too packed inside so we stood on the pavement drinking our pints. As we were stood talking and supping our beer, a mob of about 50 lads came round the corner, none of them wearing colours, all of them looking like they were going to kick off any second. Obviously Geordies. Even though they looked like they were about to come steaming into the pub we were stood outside, with no Old Bill about, for some reason I didn't give a fuck and just ignored them. I was there to watch England, so bollocks to Tyne and Wear rivalry, because I wasn't going to take sides in someone else's argument. Not that they would have seen it like that. A dozen or so non-Mackems outside one of the main Sunderland pubs wouldn't have stopped them getting stuck into anyone in their way. Nothing happened, and they were soon followed by loads of coppers, then there was the sound of more police sirens going off down the road.

It was soon time for the match so we headed off over the Wearmouth bridge towards the stadium. We found our turnstile and soon got to our seats, right at the back of the corner section. Like I say, I'd never been to Sunderland's new stadium, although I'd been to Roker Park a couple of times, and was impressed with the Stadium Of Light, even if the name's a bit shite and is easy to take the piss out of. The thing that bugged me was the amount of people wearing Sunderland shirts at the match. Yes they support Sunderland, yes we were at Sunderland's stadium, yes their leading goalscorer Kevin Phillips was in the England team, but this was an England match. Not Sunderland, England.

I've nothing against Sunderland, or Newcastle for that matter, but it seems that on the rare occasions when England play in club stadiums as opposed to Wembley, far too many fans are obsessed with slagging off their rival clubs or supporting only the one or two players in the England team that also play for their club. It may be that I'm not the same because, supporting Darlington, I don't get the opportunity to see England matches at my home ground, or Darlo players in the England team, but there's a definite change of atmosphere when England play at club stadiums.

I saw the same thing at Leeds in 1995 against Sweden, when a lot of people seemed more interested in slagging off Man Utd than watching the game (not that I was complaining on that occasion). The best atmosphere in and around England matches is certainly at the away matches, when it's mainly a case of England United. Anyway, at Sunderland I was just more determined than usual to get behind England, being as loud and patriotic as possible.

The National Anthem was sung as fervently as ever (certainly by me and Daz, anyway!), and then the match was underway. England played quite promising to start with, and took the lead early on when Alan Shearer scored from close range down the other end of the ground, prompting the usual celebrations on my behalf. Everyone else seemed a bit tame, as if they were the Premier League stand up and applaud a goal supporters. Not me, it might just be a friendly, but it's England and we'd scored. Goals have to be celebrated properly when you're at a match, not just a quick cheer and applause for ten seconds, as if sat in front of a TV screen.

Belgium soon got back into it though and were level within ten minutes. Bugger. The rest of the first half was fairly even, and it ended 1-1. Time for beer. That's what I do like about these big Premiership stadiums, bars inside the stands that serve beer at half-time, which is a bit rare in the Third Division. I had to wait fucking ages to get served, so I got two pints, and downed them both in about five minutes while watching the start of the second half on the screen just inside the stand.

After my refreshments, I joined the others back up in the seats and settled down for the rest of the second half. The match wasn't anything special, but there were some promising signs, especially from Frank Lampard of West Ham who was making his full England debut. Midway through the half, Kevin Phillips came off to thunderous applause from the England / Sunderland support, and was replaced by Michael Owen, who had been out injured for some time and he also got a good reception from the fans.

Owen played well in the short time that he was on, just to show us all what England had been missing. England's winner came from Jamie Redknapp, who hit an unstoppable shot from 25 yards into the top corner. This prompted more of the usual celebrations, followed by a rendition of "You're not singing anymore!", aimed at the 250 Belgian fans sat about 40 yards away from us. They responded with "You only sing when you're winning!"

Cheeky twats. They've got two languages of their own, so why sing in our language? Yes, I know, so we'll understand them, but they sing at their own club matches and other internationals in English. Anyway, my immediate response (accompanied by the few hundred others around me) was "Who the fucking hell are you, who the fucking hell are you?!", which seemed to shut them up! After that, the match soon finished and we were on our way out of the stadium. Not a great match, but we'd won.

Once we'd found Adrian after losing him for ten minutes, we went back to the City Tavern that we'd been in earlier. Most people in there were Sunderland fans singing about how much they hate Geordies, but we were okay and settled down for a few beers. We got talking to a Cockney bloke who had his kids with him, and when I asked where he was from he said Hartlepool. Since moving there three years ago, he'd been told to hate Darlo. Wanker. When he said he'd gone to Bulgaria in the summer it suddenly clicked that he was the Cockney from Hartlepool that Baggy had seen gobbing off about Darlo. Soon shut up when Baggy had a word with him, and he wasn't being cocky with us either. Still a wanker though, living in that piss hole and liking it. Fucking weirdo. We got on okay with him though, despite his unfortunate place of residence in the land of scum.

We then got talking to three Mackems, who upon hearing that we were Darlo fans accused us of teaming up with the Geordies all the time. We said that's bollocks and didn't know what they were on about, and then had a good laugh with them for ten minutes before rushing off to get our train.

When we got into the station, we heard a load of singing coming from down on the platform area, and as we got nearer we could hear that it was "We hate Darlo, and we hate Darlo!" Obviously monkey hangers. As we got to the stairs going down to the platform, we saw that there were about 25 Hartlepool lads, all making everyone know how much they hate us. So, with numbers of four against 25, I said "Better keep quiet, lads", to the other three.

We walked down and our train was waiting, so we headed straight for the door. Now, all day I'd been wearing a white t-shirt which had 'Darlington FC' embroidered on it in small writing and to the side. My coat was partially done up, so I didn't imagine that any of the scum would have spotted it. But they did. Once on the train, we saw that there were no seats so Adrian went for piss, Daz stood by one door, Shaun fucked off to another carriage, and I stood facing the door we'd just come through.

I was stood there, quite pissed, waiting for the doors to shut and the train to go, when suddenly a punch comes flying out of nowhere into my mouth. Didn't knock me down, but quite a hard punch. Some twat then legged it off the train, and I tried kicking him but only just caught the cunt. I went after him, but two coppers stopped me as I got to the doors and asked what happened, so I said "Some monkey hanger has just chinned us."

I was then pushed back onto the train before I could get the chance to go steaming in psychotically towards a mob of chimp-chokers. The doors shut and some Cockneys on the train said how fucked my lip was. Which was no lie, because a lump of my lip was hanging loose, and I couldn't work out whether it came from the upper or lower lip. There was blood down my face, down my t-shirt, coat, jeans, all over Adrian (he came out of the bog as it happened), on the floor, wall and ceiling! It was only one punch and it didn't put me down, but it did damage, so the cunt must have been wearing a ring or something. I was fucking fuming. The soft cunt had waited until I wasn't looking, says nothing, punches me, sees that I don't go down, then legs it off the train to join his 25 mates.

If the train doors had stopped him getting off there would have been more than my blood staining the train interior, that's for sure. The cod-headed, scaley-backed, chimp-choking, gibbon-garotting, ape-dangling, monkey-hanging fucking scum bastard! And what was I saying earlier about club rivalries at England matches?!

Once back in Northallerton, I had to have five stitches in my lips. Looked fucking lovely that did! My bird played hell, my dad wasn't impressed, and my mum spent all week laughing at my swollen lips! Still, a few months later I got awarded £1,500 compensation from the taxpayer, seeing as it's left a slight scar! Doesn't really notice much now. But I will certainly have to return the favour some time, that's all I'll say on that! The tables were turned later on in the season though. A few months later, some Pooly got done over at Kings Cross, York, and Darlington stations by Darlo, after both teams had played in London on the same day.

Back to England, and despite feeling like Frankenstein for a few days, I had the important matter of the draw for the play-offs to think about. After France qualified automatically as the best runners-up (lucky fuckers, they could also have gone out on the last day of qualifiers), the eight teams in the play-offs were England, Scotland, Ireland, Denmark, Turkey, Ukraine, Slovenia and, er, Israel. What the fuck Israel are doing in a European tournament, I don't know! Might as well have the Ivory Coast and Afghanistan in the tournament!

They'd be an easy tie though, as would Slovenia. Didn't fancy Ukraine or Denmark too much, or even Turkey after our unconvincing qualifying campaign. Scotland or Ireland? We'd never hear the end of it if we lost to either of those, especially the Jocks, but it'd be a great away trip, and I was sure we'd beat them.

The draw was finally made and we got paired up with Scotland, thus starting four weeks of hype in all the media. Now this would have been a perfect opportunity to go and see England stuff the Jocks in their own backyard, as well as have a good day out, seeing as it's only about 150 miles from where I live to Glasgow. The thing was, I was engaged at the time, on the verge of buying a house and had fuck all money saved up. I couldn't even afford a day out north of the border to see England take on Scotland. I was well fucked off, and am even more fucked off now that I'm no longer engaged! Oh well, it would be a couple of good piss ups down the pub.

The Battle of Britain

(Jamie)

AFTER A MONTH OF waiting, it was finally time for the first of the two games against Scotland to decide who would qualify for the finals of the 2000 European Championships. Like I've said, I was unable to go to this one (probably wouldn't have got a ticket anyway), so I ended up watching it up in Carlisle (where my ex lives) in the pub with a lad called Sean and his mates. I was confident that we'd beat the Jocks one or two nil, and follow it up with an easy win at Wembley the following Wednesday. When the national anthems were played, the sweaty socks (Jocks) booed like fuck at *God Save The Queen*, and it couldn't be heard at all. This seems at bit strange given that it's also the British national anthem, they're British (at the moment), and a week earlier at the Old Firm match, thousands would have been singing it themselves as passionately as we do (the Rangers fans). Wankers.

Once the match was underway, England played well and took the lead early on when Paul Scholes took the piss out of Colin Hendry before firing home into the corner of the goal. Yeeeaaasss! The pub went mental, but not as mental as the 6,000 or so English at Hampden Park. Scotland nearly equalised straight away, but shortly before half-time we were 2-0 up after another goal from Scholes, this time a header. Get in! England were cruising towards the Euro 2000 finals.

The second half was a bit of a non-event, with neither side creating much, although we could have gone 3-0 up when Andy Cole narrowly missed a decent chance. Still, a final score of 2-0 on their patch was a decent result, leaving us with an easy job the following Wednesday at Wembley.

The atmosphere at Hampden sounded brilliant, with the constant singing of *The Great Escape*, "Scotland's staying home!" to the tune of *Football's Coming Home*, and "Can you hear the Scotland sing?", being met by pure silence from the Jocks. Wish I was there! The rest of the night was spent getting pissed, toasting St George, and singing, "Can you hear the Scotland sing, no, no, can you hear the Scotland sing, no, no, can you hear the Scotland sing, 'cos I can't hear a fucking thing . . ."

In the build up to the second leg of the play-off, I heard a great joke. Kevin Keegan is getting the players ready for the England v

Scotland match, and says, "Look lads, I know it's only Scotland, easy win and that, but we've got to play the game".

Michael Owen shouts out "I'll tell you what boss, I'll take them on by myself."

Keegan has a quick think about this and agrees with Owen. So on the night of the match, Michael Owen runs out of the tunnel to take on Scotland by himself. Meanwhile, Kev Keegan takes the rest of the players down to the pub for a few beers. After about ten minutes, Alan Shearer shouts out, "Hey lads, we'd better see what the score is," so he gets the TV control, puts on Teletext, and the score comes up:

England 1 Scotland 0 (Owen, 10 minutes).

At this, a big cheer comes from the players who then continue with their drinks. Later on, Shearer shouts out, "We'd better check the score, it's nearly full-time", so he gets the control, puts on Teletext and the score comes up:

England 1 Scotland 1 (Collins 89 minutes).

The players are shocked. "Shit, what's going on?" says Tony Adams. "We'd better get down there and help out for the last few minutes."

So Keegan and the players all rush back to Wembley, but when they get there it's too late, the match has finished 1-1, and they find Michael Owen sat in the dressing room, with his head in his hands, looking devastated.

"What's up Michael? What went wrong?", asks Keegan.

"I'm sorry boss", says Owen. "I got sent off in the 11th minute."

Funny as fuck! We were so confident after the first game that the match at Wembley would be a formality. It turned out that the joke would have a touch of irony about it.

England v Scotland

(Matt)

GOD BLESS SWEDEN! Earlier in the year, I was really offended by those IKEA adverts with the slogan "Don't be so English", but all is forgiven now. I never thought they would do us a favour and beat Poland. Although can I suggest that after the performance by England at home to Scotland that the next IKEA advert with the slogan "Stop being so English" should feature a bunch of overpaid footballers on a pitch trying feebly to pass to each other.

The next day at work a Swedish colleague said to me, "I'm really glad we did you a favour. But England are fucking crap, you even lose to Scotland."

Fair enough. I couldn't really argue with that.

The week had started well with the heartbreaking news that ticket touts had suffered a major loss over the weekend. Because of the 2-0 win at Hampden, black market tickets had gone down from as much as £750 to £150. One ticket tout was quoted as saying, "I've lost a fortune this weekend. I'll be lucky to get £150 a ticket which is less than what I paid for them."

That story really brings a tear to my eye. Why do bad things happen to good people? Serves the cunt right. I hope his week got worse.

My ticket had cost me £15 from the England Members club. I had applied for it four months previously when it looked unlikely that we'd even qualify for the play-offs. Even so I thought it would be against a team like Slovenia or Ukraine. I had no idea I would be applying for a match against Scotland.

Whilst on the subject of tickets, I can't believe the cheek of some Scotland fans, and in particular the *Daily Record*, Scottish sister paper of the *Daily Mirror*. They're reporting the FA to the Commission For Racial Equality because anyone with a Scottish accent was not allowed to obtain tickets for the English section in this match. Racism! Are they taking the piss? If that's the case then we should report the whole of Scotland to the Commission For Racial Equality for racism towards the English. For once the FA are absolutely right. Of course the Scots shouldn't be allowed to obtain tickets in our section. They've been allocated 8,000 for the away end. The rest is purely for England fans. So fuck off you whinging Jocks.

Accusing the English of racism is getting tiresome, and is just becoming an excuse for people who can't get their own way. I'm sure there must have been a time when the word "racism" used to represent people who thought others were inferior because of their skin colour. If the Commission For Racial Equality had any sense then they'd send back their claim and tell them to stop wasting their time.

I had to laugh though when I read a quote from one fan in the paper who tried to obtain tickets over the phone. "When I finally got through they refused to sell me a ticket because they said I had a Scottish accent. But I'm not Scottish, I'm German."

Good. You can't come either.

On the day of the match I was down in the West End of London, so I thought I would take a walk around to Trafalgar Square, and see what was happening. It was full of Jocks, all getting pissed around Nelson's Column. The tourists didn't know what to make of it. So good are Scots at living up to their own stereotypes (wearing kilts, being drunk by midday, pissing in the street, falling over, ginger wigs, bagpipes, etc.,) that some must have thought that they had been laid on as entertainment by the British Tourist Board.

As I was wearing a hat with a St. George's cross on it I wasn't prepared to hang around. I was hoping that by the evening, Trafalgar Square would be full of English, celebrating qualification to Euro 2000. I headed off back to North London where I would meet my mate, Andrew, who also had a ticket. Andrew's family roots are Greek Cypriot, so when it comes to nationality he considers himself British rather then English, although on occasions like this he's fully behind England. If Cyprus had qualified for the play-offs which they nearly did (just lost out to Israel for second place in their group) and were drawn against England, he would have chosen to support Cyprus.

One thing we were both agreed on was what are Israel and Turkey doing in the European Championships anyway? Neither are European. I can understand that Israel does not have a very good relationship with neighbouring countries, but that doesn't hide the fact that they're not European. Unless we rename the tournament The European Championships And Friends they shouldn't be there.

I know a lot of England fans don't like Ireland, but I was hoping that they would win their play-off match against Turkey, as Ireland are a fully European state, unlike Turkey. Andrew being a 'Kip' had particularly strong feelings on that one.

We set off for Wembley at around 4pm. We wanted to get there early in order to catch the Wembley Arena box office before it shut. We had bought tickets over the phone to see Madness play in December, but they sent us numbered seats instead of standing ones which we had asked for. But once we finally got there we were told our tickets were non-transferable and that all standing was sold out. Wankers.

We now had nearly three hours to kill before kick-off. Normally that time would be killed in a nearby pub, but anyone who's ever been to Wembley will know that Wembley is the worst place in London for pubs. In fact Wembley is the worst place in London. It's a right fucking dump, just like the rest of North West London.

Bearing in mind that the areas surrounding Wembley are similar

53

shitholes, our best bet was to get a few cans from the off-licence and hang around Wembley Way until kick-off. This had been the week when the design plans for the new Wembley Stadium had been revealed. The main focal point being a giant arch to replace the Twin Towers. A lot of fuss has been made about the demolition of the Twin Towers, and I can't help feeling the same way. They are still an awesome sight as you walk out of the tube station and down Wembley Way. I understand that they have to be knocked down to accommodate a larger stadium, but why not build another set of towers that are twice the size of the present ones. Maybe with a giant arch going over the top?

As we sat down on a brick wall on Wembley Way, we watched the thousands of fans walk by. Most of them cold but in good spirit. Along with the chill factor the temperature had dropped to minus three degrees. But that didn't stop the Tartan Army wearing kilts. You could also spot the Northerners. They were the ones wearing the t-shirts! Fucking madmen. The Jocks were in optimistic mood singing, "2-0, we'll win on penalties!" and "We're gonna win 3-0!"

As kick-off approached I was feeling on edge. It didn't feel like the game was going to be a formality like everyone assumed it would be. You could sense that Scotland might have a surprise for us.

One Scotland fan had the cheek to offer me £50 for my ticket. "You must be joking," I replied.

One of the funniest things I saw was a Jock trying to take a piss in a urinal with a kilt on. You'd have thought by now they would have put zips in them. It reminded me of a time when I was in St. Paul's Cathedral and saw a vicar with a similar problem.

We took our place in the stadium when the beer had run dry. We were just behind the front row of the tunnel end, and got a thumbs up from Kevin Keegan as he walked past us. Before the game there had been a lot of speculation about the amount of respect shown during the national anthems at these fixtures. The Scottish had drowned out *God Save The Queen* at Hampden Park on Saturday. The English were being urged to show more respect, but as expected it was met with the same response. Was I one of the people who booed the Scottish national anthem? Damn right I was! They deserve it.

I don't accept all that crap about how it will inspire Scotland. If any one of those players was not already as fired up as they possibly could be, then what the fuck were they doing on the pitch for an England v Scotland game?

God Save The Queen was sung enthusiastically, if a little out of

54

tune by the home support. I can't help feeling that it's time to change our national anthem from *God Save The Queen* to something like *Land Of Hope And Glory* or *Jerusalem*. Especially for when England represents itself and not Britain. *God Save The Queen* is the British national anthem, and I'm sure that the majority of England fans consider themselves English ahead of British. I'm not a Republican, and I don't think I speak for the majority of England fans, but why sing the praises of someone who's only ever bothered to turn up to one football match in the last 34 years anyway? I just feel that an anthem like *Jerusalem* would fill people with more pride, as the main focus is on England as a country.

But anyway, the match kicked off and the stadium announcer made a number of pleas for everyone to sit down. But he was wasting his time. This was England v Scotland. Tensions are too high. Scotland were the more composed side, and even began to control the match. There was a strange atmosphere about the place. The crowd were not as loud as they could have been and the players looked like they had no confidence. You wouldn't have thought we had just come off the back of a 2-0 first leg win up at Hampden Park. Our passing was shocking, and I only recall one decent effort on goal in the first half, although we seemed to have a goal disallowed for no obvious reason. But as long as it was 0-0, it didn't really matter.

Then it came. Don Hutchinson (dirty bastard who nearly broke Manu Petit's leg) rose above the England defence and headed past Seaman. The 8,000 Jocks went mad. I had a bad feeling before the game, but by this point I was a total bag of nerves. During the half-time break all I could think about was the possibility of Scotland scoring a second. If they did, I could see them winning outright. A total humiliation that would never be lived down. Especially with the amount of Jocks who live in London (albeit on street corners).

This was Keegan's chance to prove that he knew how to turn things around at half-time. As the second half kicked off, I soon realised that we couldn't get any worse. Mind you we didn't get much better either, and the second half followed the same pattern as the first. Scotland were still the more composed side although they didn't really create enough chances to scare us. That was until the 79th minute when Tony Adams made a life saving tackle on John Collins who was through on goal. And from the resulting corner David Seaman somehow stopped a powerful header that was heading straight for the top corner. The Arsenal defence to the rescue. By this stage I didn't care about beating Scotland. Or even drawing with them. All I cared about was qualifying to Euro 2000.

The last ten minutes went by without too many scares. I was impressed with Beckham's work rate back in defence. He doesn't seem to have much impact up front at the moment, but it's not through lack of effort.

Despite the possibility of there being extra time and penalties, there's always one bloke who leaves before the end. The bloke in front of me got up and left with two minutes still on the clock! When you're in the cinema, do you leave before the end of the film? These people don't deserve their tickets.

The final whistle was met with half-hearted celebrations. But it felt like heaven compared to the feeling after the 0-0 draw in Warsaw. There and then it seemed all over, and when I look back I can't believe we've actually qualified.

Credit where credit's due and fair play to the 8,000 travelling Scots who long after the final whistle were still jumping and singing. I've got a feeling that if it were us who had lost then it would be straight down Trafalgar Square for a fight with the riot police. It was in fact Trafalgar Square where I ended up after the match (not for a fight of course). I was not in the mood for going home, and was curious to see if there were any kind of celebrations going on. All I found though was about 200 pissed up teenagers on Nelson's Column, trying to provoke the police. They were a right bunch of pricks. They even started chucking bottles at passers-by. I had no intention of joining them so I just stood by the railings and got chatting to a couple of Leeds fans.

I then noticed that one of the knobheads on Nelson's Column was calling me a wanker, and giving me the V-sign. "He can't be aiming that at me," I thought. After all, I was wearing a hat with a St George's Cross on it. Are they so desperate for a fight that they're going to start on fellow England fans?

He then pointed at me as if to say, "Yes, you."

I stared him out, then invited him to come over and say it to my face. But he was such a hard man, he shied away and turned his attention elsewhere. It's a good job he did, because if he had of come over and tried something, I would have kicked the cunt's head in. Instead I just gave him the Nescafé handshake and a one finger salute.

There was nothing worth hanging around for, plus there was a meteor shower that night that was set to peak at 2am, so I headed for home. As I live on a hill with the view of London in front of me, I would be in prime viewing territory.

I'm writing this six months before the European Championships kicks off. At this stage it is very hard to say how England will do. The Scotland home match made it clear that the slogan, "Stop Being So English", really means "Stop Being So Crap At Football". If we don't progress on how we are now, then we will be knocked out in the first round, no matter who the opposition are.

But I've got I funny feeling that this home defeat by Scotland might be a blessing in disguise. We always go into tournaments over confident and with massive expectations. And as we all know, we've only ever won the one trophy.

This time no one seems at all optimistic about our chances for Euro 2000. I like the idea of us going into this tournament as dark horses. That might work in our favour. We're fully aware of our weaknesses, and we've got six months to work on them. Keegan has not yet proven himself as coach of England and it does worry me that we can't seem to raise our game when it really matters i.e. at home to Scotland and Sweden and away to Poland and Bulgaria. But I think it's his players who have been letting him down.

From a personal point of view, I'm just happy to be there. After Warsaw I said that I'd settle for being knocked out in the first round, losing all three games. Just so long as we're represented. Not to qualify for these finals would have been a disgrace to English football, although I'm sure that as the tournament gets nearer, my hopes will become more ambitious.

I intend to travel to Holland and Belgium for about two or three weeks. If I'm not allowed to take the time off work then I will leave my job, like I did before for France 98. And that was worth every minute. Whatever happens on the pitch, I'm sure we'll have the time of our lives off it, in celebrating in the way that only England's travelling army knows how. Despite what the newspapers or anyone else might think of us, following England abroad is always a great laugh, and if they want to label us all thugs then that's their problem.

There will be a large hooligan presence out there. But they will be from all over Europe, especially from Germany, and the two host countries. Although as most fans will be staying in Amsterdam, I think they'll all be too stoned to start any trouble! They'll all be sitting in coffee shops with half closed eyes and open mouths. It was a secret ploy from UEFA all along to combat football hooliganism!

Anyway all I can do is look forward to June and July. I hope by that time I will be quietly confident. I think Kevin Keegan already is. There are no outstanding teams in Europe right now and any team with the likes of Michael Owen, David Beckham, Tony Adams, Sol

Campbell, etc., must have some sort of chance. Anyway we'll all find out in the summer. I'm off to learn some Flemish.

By the way, when it came down to that meteor shower, I never saw a thing. Fucking clouds.

The Build Up

(Jamie)

AFTER COMPLETING PART two of The Great Escape, we could now turn our attention towards the build up towards the finals. This began with the draw, which was conducted a couple of weeks before Christmas. A rather dubious seeding method was used for this, with the 16 competing teams grouped into four pots of seeds, with each of the four groups to consist of one team from each of the four pots. The tops seeds were Holland, Belgium, Germany and Spain, and England were left in the fourth pot of seeds, meaning that we'd be likely to have a difficult group to qualify from.

Having said that, all 16 nations that qualify for the European Championships are usually good sides, and we'd have to beat the best at some point if we were to win the tournament. The draw was finally made, and the groups for the first round of the finals of Euro 2000 lined up as follows:

Group A: **England**, Germany, Portugal, Romania.
Group B: Belgium, Italy, Sweden, Turkey.
Group C: Spain, Norway, Yugoslavia, Slovenia.
Group D: Holland, Denmark, France, Czech Republic.

Our group certainly couldn't be described as easy, but then none of the groups could. We were happy that we'd avoided Group D, which looked to be the toughest of the four groups. Holland would be hard to beat, especially on home soil, France are World Champions, painful though it is to say, Denmark are a decent side, having won the tournament in 1992, and the Czech Republic had a near perfect qualifying campaign, as well as reaching the final of Euro 96 in England.

Group B wasn't quite as difficult, but still contains Sweden, who have beaten us and walked away with the qualifying group in the end, and Italy, who are always a good side. Turkey never play well in big tournaments or away from home, and Belgium, although the hosts and having improved slightly over the last couple of years, were picked out as the other likely first round casualty of the group.

Group C contained perhaps the weakest of the qualifiers, Slovenia, but they did beat Ukraine in the play-offs so could not be written off completely. Spain are a decent side, but they always under-perform in tournaments. Norway are another good side, capable of beating anyone on their day, and I thought they'd go through from the group. Yugoslavia have a lot of good players and were probably 50-50 with Spain for second place behind Norway in my opinion.

Which leaves us with England's group. We'd been drawn against Germany in the World Cup 2002 qualifiers a week earlier, so the media were loving it when we got drawn against the Germans again. After they'd beaten us on penalties in Euro '96 in England, the 1990 World Cup in Italy, and beat us 3-2 in Mexico in the 1970 World Cup, we would finally have the chance to beat the Krauts and show them who was number one (not just at war!). Well, we'd have three chances actually, but it was crucial that we started off our two year competitive rivalry against them with a win at Euro 2000 and progression to the quarter-finals.

After being beaten 3-0 by Croatia in the 1998 World Cup, and struggling to overcome Turkey in the Euro 2000 qualifying group, Germany were not the side they used to be. They seemed to have too many ageing players and not enough young quality players coming through. They can never be written off though, as previous tournaments have illustrated. At least our group game against them wouldn't be decided on penalties! Of the other two teams, Romania beat us in the 1998 World Cup, although again perhaps they have too many ageing players, and Portugal never seem to do much in major tournaments. I was reasonably confident that England would qualify for the quarter-finals, along with Germany or possibly Portugal.

In January, we received the ticket application information from the England Members Club, which was set up by the Football Association as the official and only outlet for tickets for England away games. As mentioned by Matt earlier, in early 1999, they had announced the creation of a 'loyalty points' system, whereby members are allocated points for attending certain matches. Any away match gives you three points, home friendlies two points, home qualifiers one point. In addition to this, people who have been continuous members since 1990/91 get three extra points, since 1992/96 two extra points, since 1997/98, one extra point.

It was decided that when allocating tickets for the finals, members with ten or more points would be allocated tickets for all three group games, members with less than ten points would only get one ticket allocated, and tickets for the knockout stages if England progressed would be allocated on a priority basis according to points accumulated.

Now, it's all very well having a loyalty points system which gives priority over tickets in short supply to members who have attended more matches, but this system contains a lot of imperfections. Firstly, only matches within the current membership period but up to the England v Scotland play-off (not including the away match in Glasgow?!) counted towards any loyalty points. In the 1999-2000 membership period, I'd been to England v Sweden (one point), Poland v England (three points), England v Belgium (two points), and had two points for being a continuous member since 1993, giving me a grand total of eight points.

Yet in January 2000, we were being invited to apply for tickets for the finals of the 2000 European Championships, the qualifiers for which began in September, 1998. I attended two away matches in the autumn of 1998, in Sweden and Luxemburg, both qualifying matches for the finals of the 2000 European Championships, at a combined cost of about £600. And now the FA were telling me that this counts for absolutely sweet FA (that's fuck all!) when applying for tickets for the Euro 2000 finals! I've been to three of the four away qualifiers, yet I was being offered one fucking ticket for the finals, when someone who lives in London, pays £5 on the tube to get to Wembley, went to all of 1999's home games, has been a member since 1996, but has never left this country to follow England, gets priority over me! How the fuck is that rewarding loyalty?

All matches for Euro 2000 should count, not just those in the current membership period. It seemed funny that they didn't allocate points for the Scotland away match (not even two points as a one off measure), when it was further away than the Wembley leg for those members in the South East to travel to. Yet when it comes to matches at Wembley, which would cost me over £50 on the train (plus beer!) and two days off work for evening matches (last train home leaves before kick-off!), they happily give out points to their loyal Wembley following. Never mind those of us that have travelled all over Europe following England in the qualifiers. What a fucking piss take!

I should get more points than someone who's been a member since 1996, someone who's been a member since 1990 should get more than three points, any away match should get more than three points, with matches in scummy places like Poland, Moldova or Albania attracting bonus points. And above all, when allocating tickets for a major tournament, be it the World Cup or European Championships, all matches since that tournament's qualifying matches began should count towards 'loyalty' points.

In contrast to me, Matt managed to get ten points, having been a member since 1998 (one point) and been to England v Poland (one point), England v Sweden (one point), England v Luxemburg (one point), Poland v England (three points), England v Scotland (one point) and having a ticket for but not attending England v Belgium (two points)! Like I say, it's okay for those within easy reach of London. Having said that, with Wembley being refurbished and England playing home matches around the north of England or the Midlands, people like me will have the advantage. And at least the FA are doing something about this little anomaly, by making all games from the autumn of 2000 count towards tickets for the 2002 World Cup, assuming we qualify. But those that run the game of football, both here and abroad, seem more concerned with sponsors and corporate entertainment than the real supporters like myself who travel around their country for their club and around their continent for their country.

Still, one ticket or whatever, I'd be going over to Holland and Belgium for the duration. If I couldn't get tickets outside the stadiums for a decent price, I'd just watch the matches in a bar somewhere, as I'd mostly done in France at the World Cup. The plan was to go over on the ferry from Hull to Rotterdam on the 10th of June, two days before England v Portugal in Eindhoven. Me and Matt would be going until England won the tournament or got knocked out, Mel and Daz would come with us but return after a week, and Sven and Jon (Sunderland fans from Northallerton who we'd met up with in France - see my first book, *Toulouse Or Not To Lose!*) would be going for two weeks, along with a few others. Baggy was also going, with a few mates from the Leeds area, and we'd try and meet up with them over there.

The first of England's friendly matches in the build up to Euro 2000 was at home to Argentina in February. Neither me or Matt went to that one (Matt was in New York!), so I just watched it at home on the telly. I'd forgotten just how much I hate the Argies. I don't really mean that in a racist sense, but my dislike of particular nations is based on football and the level of hatred they aim towards us, hence Argentina and Wales are not exactly two of my favourite countries!

When it comes to football, Argentina are such a bunch of dirty, cheating bastards, diving and play acting, and using their hands to play a game that is not called football for no reason. They cheated us out of the 1986 World Cup (Maradonna's handball 'goal'), they cheated us out of the 1998 World Cup (dodgy penalty, dodgy sending off, disallowed goal, another handball), and were dirty bastards when we knocked them out of the World Cup in 1966, but that was a bit before my time.

With Michael Owen and Robbie Fowler out injured, Keegan decided to give Emile Heskey his chance in the starting line up. Although I've always thought he's a decent player, I wasn't sure if he'd be good enough for England, but he had a brilliant game and got a well deserved man of the match award. The Argies didn't know what to do with him. The defence looked solid, Jason Wilcox did quite well on the left wing (for a change we had a left footed player on the left), and Dennis Wise played well in central midfield. The substitutes that came on all played well, particularly Kevin Phillips and Andy Cole who livened up the game for the last ten minutes.

Shearer was tripped when clean through on goal and should have had a penalty, but along with Paul Scholes I thought he had a fairly quiet game. True to form, the Argies managed a blatant handball, although this time it was just on the halfway line. Overall though, especially after the Scotland at home performance, I thought we played well and were unlucky not to win. As much as I dislike them, Argentina are one of the best football sides in the world, but were made to look quite ordinary on the night. The only bad point was the announcement a few days later that Alan Shearer was to retire from international football after Euro 2000. I still say he's the best striker we've got at international level, even if he doesn't always warrant automatic selection for every match. Having said that, like he says himself, it gives us time to explore other options up front before the 2002 World Cup.

On the domestic front, both myself and Matt suffered defeat in finals for our respective clubs. Darlington lost 1-0 to Peterborough at Wembley in the Division Three play-off final, after beating the scum from Hartlepool (home and away) in the semi-finals. I was absolutely gutted after that. Beating the scum isn't much consolation for losing out on promotion when we'd been in the top three for half of the season, but it did help, knowing how humiliated they must have felt after we beat them 2-0 and 1-0. Oh well, back to the Third Division and the joys of Rochdale, Hull, Barnet and all, after Euro 2000.

Arsenal lost in the UEFA Cup final to Galatasaray of Turkey, losing on penalties after a 0-0 draw. Before the match there was a good few hours battling in the streets of Copenhagen where the match was being played, this less than a month after two Leeds fans got stabbed to death in Istanbul before playing Galatasary. I was sickened by what happened to the two Leeds lads. What made it worse was wankers in the media suggesting that the Leeds fans were being 'culturally insensitive'. What fucking bollocks. No one deserves to die because of football, especially being stabbed 17 times like one of the Leeds lads was.

Whatever happened that night, whatever the small group of Leeds fans might have been doing (singing and drinking?), it did not warrant a group of Turks going in with their knives with the intention to kill. They were at it again in Copenhagen, stabbing an Arsenal fan, although luckily he was okay. After those events, the Turks that got done over fucking deserved it. I know that sounds simplistic and small minded, but having travelled all over with Darlo and England, and seen the shit that happens to English football fans abroad, and the shit that our media write about us, and the way that some of the Turks behave, I have no sympathy for any Turk getting a good kicking after what they'd done.

The thing about all that though was that it wound things up for Euro 2000. With the amount of Turks living in all European cities, something was bound to go off at Euro 2000 with them. It certainly made me more apprehensive about going over there. It's okay when you're in a big group, but I was expecting it to get dodgy when there's just two of us in Brussels and we're away from the crowds. Nothing would put me off though, and I would get stuck in if I had to.

I was really looking forward to going overseas again, with the army of St George, and with the Third Division finally over for another three months it was time to get ready to Euro 2000.

The first of three warm up games in the fortnight before the finals was against Brazil at Wembley, the day after Darlo's defeat against Peterborough. The media were coming out with the usual hype about how Brazil are the best team in the world, which I suppose they probably are. I didn't go to the match despite staying over in London that weekend, although a few of the lads we went down with did go. I watched a bit of the match in a pub near Kings Cross, before going over to meet the others for the bus back home.

From what I saw, England played fairly well with Michael Owen putting us 1-0 up after half an hour, but then Brazil equalised with a bit of a soft goal just before half-time. By all accounts the second half wasn't up to much, although it was described by some as a solid performance. I didn't really have the stomach for football that day after the previous night's events!

Four days later and England played their last warm up game at Wembley before Euro 2000, which was also Alan Shearer's last game for England at Wembley. The opposition was Ukraine, who must surely be the best team not to qualify for Euro 2000, having been beaten by Slovenia in the play-offs. With my departure for Euro 2000 only ten days away, I decided to stay in and watch this one on the telly. England played with Robbie Fowler up front alongside Alan Shearer, and Steve McManaman was included for his first England game in a while, fresh from his Champions League win with Real Madrid.

The game started off quite lively, with both sides creating chances. The only thing that worried me was the 3-5-2 formation. Playing with three central defenders meant that Beckham was having to play far too deep, and the defence looked vulnerable at times. Nigel Martyn was on great form again in goal, and with England looking more and more promising, a goal went in just before half-time, with Robbie Fowler scoring from two yards after a corner.

As the second half wore on, England played better and better, and scored the second midway through the half, Tony Adams scoring this time, again after a corner. England seemed to be taking the piss later on, which is good when playing a half decent side like Ukraine. The match finished 2-0, and afterwards the final squad of 22 was announced for Euro 2000. My only surprise was that Rio Ferdinand of West Ham had been left out.

England's last warm up game was in Malta, a week before the tournament started. I watched this one in three different pubs whilst on an all day session in York. England had a goal disallowed and then Martin Keown scored one which was allowed. Richard Wright, making his debut in goal, gave away a penalty which Malta scored from after the ref had ordered it to be retaken. England played crap, but Emile Heskey scored late on to give us a 2-1 win, despite Wright giving away another penalty which he saved. It wasn't a good game, but we'd won and the last warm up match before a major tournament is never much to get excited about.

So, with three warm up games in a week out of the way, it was finally time to focus on the Euro 2000 finals. Me, Daz and Mel would get the train from Northallerton, meeting Matt at Hull for the ferry to Rotterdam. Sven, John, Geoff, Rich, Steve and Dean (all in their early twenties and from Northallerton, were going on the day before us, as our ferry was fully booked by the time they tried to reserve tickets in February. We'd arranged to meet them in Eindhoven before the Portugal game in a pub called The Trafalgar, which is in a Euro 2000 guide book that both me and Sven had. We also arranged to meet Baggy, Ten (from Darlo), and others who were travelling with Northern Holidays to each of the first round matches. Baggy would stay on if England qualified for the later stages.

As it turned out I got one ticket for the group stages (England v Germany), and vouchers for the Quarter-final, Semi-final and Final, meaning that if England were there, I'd get a ticket after going to a voucher exchange point near the venue. Better than nothing, but I was still fucked off about the Sweden and Luxemburg away games counting for nothing. Matt had the same as me, plus tickets for the other two group games, against Portugal and Romania.

I got sick of all the shite in the media about how much trouble there would be over there. It was well over the top, and so were the preparations of the Dutch and Belgian police, not helped by that twat of a Home Secretary, Jack Straw. He kept saying that the police over there should deal with all hooligans severely. What he's saying is that all England football fans who go over there should be treated like shit by the authorities because we're all mindless scum.

The police over there were saying how they'd arrest English people for not having a passport with them at any time, not having a ticket, or for behaving aggressively. So anyone without a ticket, who has short hair and is English, has had a few beers, and sings *No Surrender* is a prime target for the local constabulary. Sounds like me and countless other fans. What fucking bollocks. Still, no matter what impression the press were giving, I was well up for it when it was time to go, ready for three weeks (hopefully) of beer, football and whatever. I'd just have to watch out for over zealous police and knife merchant Turks! But it was finally time for another tour of duty with the mighty army of St George.

Day One
Saturday 10th June

(Matt)

I'D BEEN LOOKING forward to this day for ages. France '98 had given me a real appetite for following England abroad, and I was full of optimism. Myself, Jamie, Daz and Mel had cabins booked on a ferry that would depart from Hull at around 6.30pm. We were due to arrive at the Europort near Rotterdam at around 8.30 on Sunday morning. On the pitch the optimism was no higher than it was six months previously. The team did not look like they were up to much, but we would just have to wait and see what happened. My personal tip for Euro 2000 glory was Sweden.

Thanks to a phantom appearance at the England v Belgium friendly, I had managed to get enough loyalty points to obtain tickets for all England's matches at Euro 2000. I was delighted about this, but still stand by what I said about the loyalty points system being unfair. Someone who attended the away qualifiers in Sweden, Luxemburg, and Scotland would be on less points than someone who only attended the home friendly against France. And of course there are still too many tickets handed out to corporate types. But what the fuck. I had tickets, and I wasn't complaining.

I had quit my job as a parcel worker at UPS the day before, not because I wasn't allowed the time off for Euro 2000, but because I was getting a lot of work as a film and TV extra and had to choose between the two jobs. Conveniently, I had handed in my month's notice four weeks before we were due to travel.

I set off from Kings Cross to Doncaster at around midday. Apart from passing the home of the greatest football club in the world (no, not Peterborough), there was little else to make the journey interesting, so I found a way of entertaining myself by making a list of songs that relate to either football clubs or players:

"Money For Nothing" - Darren Anderton
"Fat Bottomed Girls" - John Hartson
"I'm Bad, I'm Nationwide" - Watford
"Can't Stand Still" - Martin O' Neil
"I Am The Walrus" - Frank Clark, Harry Redknapp

"Yesterday's Men" - Middlesborough
"Turd On The Run" - Chris Sutton
"When I'm 64" - Steve Ogrisovic
"Substitute" - Teddy (you're still a reserve) Sheringham
"Monkey Man" - Martin Keown

Sorry Martin, but you do look like an angry ape at times.

Anyway, I arrived in Hull via Doncaster and met up with the others and went straight for a drink in a pub outside the station. Daz and Mel advised me to take my England baseball cap off as apparently football fans are banned from North Sea Ferries! What else are they gonna think hundreds of short haired lads with Hacket t-shirts are doing on board their ferry?

We took a taxi to the ferry port which is about three miles out of town. On the way we all agreed that none of us would be getting involved in any trouble out there. It wouldn't be worth it, and we had too much to lose. Plus we could do without appearing on the front page of The Sun.

It had been reported that day that 49 Arsenal fans, who were either season ticket holders or club members, were caught on camera fighting in Copenhagen and banned from the club for life. Obviously none of us wanted that to happen to us.

Once we arrived at the ferry port we found it was full of bikers. German bikers! Hundreds of them. We never heard them speak, nor did they have any national symbols on them, but we knew they were German. You could just tell. They were all wearing leather, as bikers would do, but the big give away was their haircuts and moustaches. All of them were doing a brilliant job of living up to German stereotypes.

After checking in, we were soon to make our way to passport control. There a man approached us and asked us if we were travelling for the football. When we said that we were, he took our passports away for inspection. They would be checking our details with the police to see if we were known hooligans. It didn't really bother us as none of us had anything to hide. Ten minutes later though, a policeman comes back with our passports and asks if he could speak to Daz.

As we knew, Daz holds a couple of 'drunk and disorderly' charges, but neither of them were related to football. The copper took him to one side and started to question him. At one stage we were worried that he would not let him travel. He was being a provocative fucker as well.

After a further ten minutes he decided that Daz would be allowed to travel. He had told him that he could have turned him away there and then, and had asked Daz to give him one reason why he shouldn't. Apparently he had already turned people away for similar offences. What a piss take. I thought this operation was to stop known hooligans from travelling to the finals. What's the point of targeting someone who has two minor offences which have nothing to do with football? The policeman had absolutely no grounds to turn him away and he knew it too.

As we boarded the ferry you could tell Daz was relieved to have been let through. At one stage it did look like he was in danger of being turned away, and Mel had said at the time that if that was to happen he wouldn't travel either. Not least because it would have meant that Mel would have to travel back by himself on the Thursday, the day when the two of them were scheduled to return home.

Once on the ferry, it was straight to the bar to get down to business, with Jamie, predictably, drinking faster than the rest of us. The boat was becoming full of German bikers. It turned out that they were all booked on our ferry. There seemed to be around 300-400 of them! "This should be interesting," we said to each other. Surprisingly, there was only a handful of England fans on board. We knew that the ferry had been fully booked for months, but just assumed that it would be full of football fans travelling to the finals. The German bikers were all coming back from some motorbike festival in the Isle Of Man.

The lot of them just made me laugh. They made the leather clad member of The Village People look heterosexual. Although I'm sure most of them were not gay, they certainly looked it. Especially one who was wearing leather dungarees and a luminous green jumper. The most popular haircut among them seemed to be the Eighties pop star look. This was accompanied by moustaches that would make Rudi Voller proud.

The ferry was delayed by a couple of hours, something about an exceptionally low tide, but we weren't complaining as it meant we'd get two more hours in bed the next morning. It was a good job as well, because the lager seemed quite strong, and the way things were going, we'd be approaching the pissed stage before the boat even started moving. We got talking to a group of Bury fans who were also travelling for the football. A few of them had charges against them which were football related, but they didn't have any trouble getting through passport control. I think mainly because the charges were about ten years old. Apparently though there was a Middlesbrough fan on board with as many as nine football related convictions to his name. He obviously didn't have any problems at passport control either.

Whilst keeping an eye on the Belgium v Sweden opening game on the TV, we got talking about what kind of hosts Holland and Belgium would be. We were confident about Holland, but not so sure about Belgium. The message that the Belgian authorities had been giving out was one of hostility. We'd seen their police in training on the news, and to say that they were up for a fight was an understatement. It also seemed that you could be nicked for something trivial like singing in the street. Jamie summed it up when he said, "The only thing Belgium's good for is hosting wars."

Good point, although at the time I thought it was a little harsh.

The ferry got moving at around 8:30pm. We went out on deck and watched the Humber Bridge fade into the distance. We were travelling the opposite way to the sun which was in perfect line with the back of the ferry. I looked down at the water, which after a while became hypnotic. I've always found it enjoyable, travelling by sea. It took a while to get out of English waters. On the way we passed an area that was just pure docklands. There were bright lights everywhere and it seemed to go on forever. It was like a city made out of cranes. I'm not sure which town it was, Jamie thought it was Immingham, but wherever, it was an incredible sight.

As we approached the North Sea we went back inside, and ended up in the ferry's small casino. We went straight for the roulette table, but I didn't bother playing as I was convinced it was a loser's game. Then Jamie ends up winning £50. It's the first time he's ever played it as well. Winning twice on the same number, 27 (his age). The lucky bastard. The Chinese woman who was in charge of the table tried to encourage him to play on, but he wasn't gonna fall for that. When they do that you know it's time to quit and take your winnings. Daz won back what he put on, while Mel lost a tenner. It was all good fun though, and I was keen to have a go on the return trip to England.

Mind you Jamie never stopped gloating about it the whole evening. We made sure that he would be buying the next round back at the bar where entertainment was being provided by a Steps cover band! Surely Steps are already a cover band for Abba anyway. They were one male member short and doing a pretty feeble job of it as well. Mind you, Mel and Daz didn't seem to mind, as they just stood by the bar and watched the whole show. They were one step away from getting on the dance floor. Myself and Jamie would make sure we took the piss out of them for that.

Rather than watch a Steps cover band with a load of German bikers, I decided to go back outside and get some fresh air. It was pitch black outside, apart from a full moon which shone on the sea. It was like looking at a painting.

As I got back inside, things were livening up as Jamie, Mel and Daz, plus the lads from Bury, got together and started singing the usual England songs. Daz asked the DJ to play either *Three Lions* or *Vindaloo*, but was told that they were not allowed to play any England songs for fear of incitement. Pathetic. We'd just have to sing it ourselves. A few of the other passengers looked a bit apprehensive about it, but we weren't hurting anyone. We were drunk, loud, and out of tune, but still managed to put on a better act than the Steps cover band from earlier. In fact we were probably better than Steps themselves.

Myself and Jamie were sat down near the bar and ended up talking to a few of the German bikers. Jamie spoke to them in German which seemed to impress them. One of the Germans on the table next to us, a fat fucker he was, turned round to me and said, "Football is a simple game, played for 90 minutes. And in the end Germany win."

"We'll see about that," was my polite response.

I was glad he said that though because if we were to beat his sausage-eating countrymen a week later it would just make victory even sweeter.

Somehow, Jamie got away with proposing a toast to Bomber Harris! I thought the Germans would go mad, but they just responded with, "Oh jah, Bomber Harris, ha ha ha!"

I'm sure they didn't understand what he meant.

As the evening wore on I decided it was time to call it a night and go back to the cabin to get some sleep. On my way I noticed that the Germans were drinking beer out of a big heavy boot that belonged to one of the bikers. It was being passed around the tables, and each one of them drunk out of it. Pretty disgusting really. The boot then made its way round to Jamie. I could just tell by the look on his face that he was gonna do something stupid. He was too drunk to think properly. I stood there helpless, but before I could shout, "Don't do it!", he picked up the big sweaty boot and poured the drink down his throat. Fucking disgusting. 5% alcohol, 30% sweat. Shame on my cousin. I would let him know about it the next day as well. I've got nothing against those German bikers, but one

71

look at them and the last thing you would want to do would be to drink out one of their boots.

Anyway, it was time to get some sleep. Mel and Daz had already retired, and not long afterwards Jamie somehow found his way to the cabin to pass out. With 400 leather clad Germans hanging around we thought it would be a good idea to lock the door. The beds in the cabin were quite comfortable so we would get a decent night's sleep. The next morning we would arrive in Holland then make our way to Eindhoven, the city where England would play their first game against Portugal.

Day Two
Sunday 11th June

(Jamie)

I WOKE UP with a steaming hangover. I couldn't remember getting back to the cabin from the bar, but could remember drinking out of a German biker's boot! Fucking disgusting. Mel had managed to puke up in one of the communal showers in the middle of the night after he couldn't find the toilets. He only remembered this happening a couple of weeks later.

After a quick wash we went up to the cafe area near the bar where we had a coffee, and talked to the Bury lads we'd been talking to the night before. They looked as fucked as I was, especially the one that was supposed to be driving.

With the final call for all foot passengers to leave the boat coming over the tannoy system, it was time to get off the ferry and go through the terminal. We were just about the last ones off the ferry, and there were no police at the terminal like we'd expected, just a chilled out Dutch passport control officer who told us to have a good time and enjoy the football. Once through there we got onto the North Sea Ferries bus which took us the 20 miles into the centre of Rotterdam, and dropped us next to Central Station.

We bought our tickets to Eindhoven, which were only about a tenner, and after getting something to eat and drink we went to the platform for our train. There were a few other English about, but not as many as I'd thought there would be. Once on the train we shared a compartment with a bloke who said he was originally from Sudan. He started talking to us about football, and said, "I think England have a bit of a problem with Turkey," to which I replied, "Yeah, just a bit."

He got off about halfway through the journey, and we arrived in Eindhoven at about midday. It was quite hot and sunny there, and although I'd phoned and reserved a hotel for us in Geldrop, a small town about three miles away, we thought about looking for a hotel in central Eindhoven until being told that everywhere was full. So we got a taxi from the station over to Geldrop, and were dropped off at our hotel.

I was a bit worried when I phoned the hotel in April because the bloke seemed so laid back. He just took my name, said "Okay", and

73

didn't want my address or phone number. So it was a relief when we got there to find that he was expecting us and had kept the rooms that I'd reserved. He was just your typical laid back Dutchman. The rooms were okay, two rooms with two beds each, and once I'd hung my Darlo flag over the balcony to accompany the Birmingham City flag a few windows away, we headed off in search of a bar.

The weird thing about Geldrop was that it was totally deserted. Sunday afternoon, just about everywhere was shut, virtually no one walking about, not even any cars, just people on bikes. The town was very smart and clean looking in appearance, and there was no local Turkish population which meant we'd be unlikely to get any hassle there.

We finally found a bar that was open and settled down outside for a few relaxing beers. It was nice there, sat in a small, quite Dutch town, chilling out in the sun, slowly drinking large glasses of Heineken (which I was asking for in Dutch - "Een grotten bier alstublieft"). By late afternoon though, it was time to get the train into Eindhoven to check out the bars down there.

The train journey into Eindhoven only lasted five minutes, and once there we found the Trafalgar pub where we'd arranged to meet the others the next day. The pub was virtually empty (it was only 5pm), but it was like an English pub and sold pints rather than half litres or even smaller. We only had the one beer there though, as we wanted to find the main square in the centre of Eindhoven.

It's always funny reading a guide book and seeing a map of a place before you go and then trying to match it all up when you're there. Eindhoven was quite straightforward in that respect compared to some other places. We soon found the square, which was a decent size, although about half the size of the square in Toulouse where we were two years earlier. The square was already quite full of English, sat around outside the various bars, and it was clear that it would be taken over by England for the next couple of days, even though the Dutch were playing their first match of the tournament that evening.

There was also a mixture of English and Dutch having a kick about in the middle of the square. Most people involved were doing a few kick ups, a header or two, then passing the ball on to someone else, but one lad would just hoof the ball in any direction without the slightest idea where it would go, although it usually ended up quite near to the TV crews that were positioned on a balcony over one of the main bars. Another lad with a Leeds shirt on had most of the square laughing when he managed to crash into a small potted conifer tree and knock it over when chasing after the ball.

It was a fairly relaxed atmosphere as we were all sat around the square, slowly drinking beer, although at one point a Turk walked through the square wearing a t-shirt with the Turkey badge on it, which resulted in everyone chanting "Scum! Scum! Scum!" at him. His pace soon quickened.

Whilst we were sat there a bloke asked if we needed tickets for the Portugal match. Matt and Daz had tickets, but me and Mel were without so bought a couple for 300 guilders each (about £85) after being taken to McDonalds to meet the person with the tickets. Two seats together in the main stand, price category 1, not a bad price really, and my winnings from the casino on the ferry went some way to covering the cost.

After that we got talking to the Birmingham City fan who was staying at our hotel and had hung his flag out of the window, but after a while we decided to check out the Irish pub called O'Shea's, just off the main square, where we had a couple of pints. It was fairly busy in there, although not packed, but soon I found that the common irritating thing about Dutch pubs is the distinct lack of tables and chairs. We ended up sitting on the floor, feeling quite knackered, and said we'd go back in there later on when the place livened up a bit.

We then headed back to the bar near the station, where we had a couple of beers and watched a bit of the football (France v Denmark). Soon got bored of that though, seeing as France were winning, and after consuming a solid beer base in McDonalds we went back to the main square.

As we were supping away on more beer, Daz spotted one of the Hull City lads who'd been on our bus to Poland, so we talked to him for a bit, mainly about a certain incident that happened when we played down there in March.

"Can we have our pool ball back?" he asked (a service bus that the coppers made us travel on back to Hull station had a pool ball thrown through the window as we passed one of their main pubs).

As I've said, Holland were playing that night, and the pub soon got quite full inside with everyone wearing orange in the way that the Dutch do. When I got a drink and asked for it in Dutch, the barman gave me an orange shirt to wear, but I declined the offer. I wanted them to win, but there was no way I was wearing that. I didn't see much of the game, but Holland won thanks to a dodgy penalty and the Dutch were happy. There were still more English around the square than Dutch though. After a while we moved on to O'Shea's again, but were told by the bouncers that it was full, so we went another 50 yards to another pub with some tables outside.

By now it was about 8pm, and we spent most of the evening at that bar. There was us four (three Darlo, one Gooner), a table of Hull, and a table of Scunthorpe, all talking about various incidents that had happened with each other over the years. The lads from Bristol on the table next to us seemed a bit left out. More and more people turned up there, and after a few more beers the singing started. All the usual stuff, *No Surrender*, *God Save The Queen*, plus the new favourites, "Singing die die Turkey fucking die!", and "Turkey where are ya?".

This was shown just over a week later on the BBC's *Panorama* programme, which was like a TV extension of the tabloids, saying what a bunch of nasty xenophobic drunken hooligans we all are. The four of us couldn't quite be seen on the programme, but we could certainly be heard along with all the others there. Anyway, for about an hour or more there was a good crowd of us stood up, drinking and singing, taking the piss out of the Dutch for us beating them 4-1 at Wembley in Euro '96, and generally having a good laugh.

The police had the right idea. They were around, driving and walking past, but never once intervened or gave us any hassle, so there was no friction and a good laugh was had by all.

When the bar had ran out of beer we all went down to the square, joining in with more chants of "Die die Turkey fucking die!", as well as "Lie down, if you love England", with 50 of us lying down and singing on the ground. After a few renditions of *Dambusters* and the accompanying outstretched arms, it was time to head back to the station to get a taxi back to Geldrop. We got a burger on the way, waited ages for a taxi, talked to some Tottenham fans who Matt decided were typical scum wide boy wankers, saw a couple of the Scunny lads again, jumped the queue and got a taxi back to our hotel. Quite a good first night in Holland, and I was impressed with Eindhoven and the Dutch.

I was woken up after a bit of sleep by the realisation that I was lying on the floor after falling out of bed. Matt was woken up by the loud thud from the other side of the room, and was chuckling away to himself. Fucking bed. Soon got back to sleep though after the amount I'd had to drink.

Day Three
Monday 12th June

(Matt)

I STARTED THE day off with a walk around Geldrop. It has to be the most quiet town I've ever been to in my whole life. It was a public holiday and the whole place was empty. Literally. Unlike Britain, the Dutch treat public holidays as a day of rest, the only movement in town being bits of litter blowing around in the light breeze. It was like a ghost town. You would think that the whole population of Geldrop had been evacuated. Maybe they heard the English were coming?

As I was stood by myself in the main street I felt like shouting out, "WHERE IS EVERYBODY?" The whole situation reminded me of the film, *The Truman Show*. I felt like I was playing the part of Truman, and that there was a film director in the background, who was about to cue the population of Geldrop to walk on set. Geldrop was a nice town, but it was just too quiet for the kind of holiday we were on.

We travelled to Eindhoven by train at about eleven in the morning. It was a 7.45pm kick-off, but we wanted to get there early to sample the atmosphere. As we walked out of Eindhoven station there was a nice relaxed atmosphere about the place. There was a band playing, and the Dutch who were all wearing orange, were joining in with the occasion and mixing well with the English. Even when Holland were not playing the Dutch still dressed up as if it were their match day. We had already come to the conclusion the day before that Holland was a good country, and that the Dutch were a brilliant race of people. They're a very friendly, easy going nation.

We made our way to the town square which was already full of English. Most people were just drinking beer and playing football. The Dutch police looked very relaxed and even seemed to be enjoying the occasion themselves. They were just walking around in twos, and I even saw a couple of them kick a football about. There were lots of television crews around, waiting to film any trouble, but they were never gonna get anything out of today.

We went for a couple of drinks in a bar off the square where we would meet up with Baggy and his mates, Andy (Leeds), Ten (Darlo), and Sour (Man U). The bar would have been alright had it

77

not been for the Dutch techno they were playing. I've heard some bad European dance music before, but this shit was just unbelievable. Full blast as well. It sounded like the sort of music that you get on a Nintendo game like *Mario Brothers*. Mario goes to Eindhoven.

We went back to the square which by this stage was completely full of English. We had totally invaded Eindhoven. Red and white everywhere. People were hanging St George's crosses wherever they could find the space. Buildings, trees, statues. It reminded us all of Toulouse from two years ago when England played Romania. There was a very similar atmosphere with no sign of trouble, and just a good feeling about the place.

A man came up to us and asked us if we wanted to have the St George's cross painted on our face. Sour obliged and had one painted on his forehead, then paid for Andy to have one done. For some reason Andy chose to have one painted on his arse! The man was quite happy to do it, but he got a few funny looks from passersby.

We then met up with Sven ad John outside the Irish bar we had been in the previous night, and they were with a few mates who I'd never seen before. One of them was telling us how he had shagged a fat Dutch girl on the top of the hotel roof in Rotterdam! He didn't seem to know if he was proud of himself or not.

The biggest flag in the square was a massive St George's cross that was draped over one of the hotels. It had Motspur Park written on it. It belonged to another lad called Daz, a Leeds fan from Motspur which I'm told is in the South West London suburbs, who Jamie would get to know a week later. At first I thought the flag read 'Hotspur' which naturally made my skin crawl.

Among other flags in the square, Millwall were quite well represented along with Coventry, and of course Villa, Birmingham, and Man City, who always have good turn outs. I also met a lot of fans from Colchester and Chesterfield. Arsenal, Man U, and Chelsea, were very poorly represented. I put that down to the fact that we've all played too many European games throughout the season. Too much travelling and too much money. Chelsea have always put out good turnouts for England, and I know that a lot of Arsenal have travelled with England. For example, due to the fact that I had no match ticket, and that my travel plans fell apart at the last minute, I never made it out to Copenhagen for the UEFA Cup final against the knife merchants from Istanbul. If I had, the whole trip would have cost me around £400-500. I then would have struggled to make it to Euro 2000. Although having said that, Leeds had a European campaign and they were well represented.

There was one Man Utd flag in the square. Quite a good one I have to admit. A St George's cross which read, Born in England, live in England, die in England. Bit like that old Texas saying, "Texas born, Texas bred, damn I'll be Texas dead". How about, "Born in Essex, live in Essex, die in Essex, support Man U"?

I noticed that there was a lot of open air portable urinals in the square and around the bars. They made me laugh because someone had actually gone to the bother of putting 'Gents' signs on them! As if any woman was going to go for a piss in the open air and in front of everyone.

There wasn't much singing going on in the square. It was a hot day and most people were just drinking beer and taking it easy. There was loud music being played in the square by the organisers, which was later claimed by *Panorama* as a ploy to drown out aggressive chanting. That claim sounds a little hollow when you know that the main MC himself started singing *No Surrender* into the microphone!

I was disgusted by the fact that there were so many people walking around wearing those plastic St George's hats which have *The Sun* and *News Of The World* written on them. After the way they slag us off, those hats should be stamped on. You walk around with those hats on giving them free advertising, and in return they'll call you scum. That doesn't sound like a very good deal to me.

We ended up around one of the main streets just off the square. There was a lane that was just full of bars and Euro 2000 banners. There were a few Portuguese about, and throughout the day the one thing I noticed about them was that they looked like the sort of tourists you get in London. Rucksacks, cameras, jester hats. It's the same with most fans of other countries when they follow their national team. With England as we know, it's mostly lads who follow the national team. The support other countries get seems to come from richer classes. If you went to a domestic league match in Spain, Italy, or Portugal, it would be a different story. Brazil spring to mind on this subject. The fans they bring to the World Cup are rich tourists. If you went to a league match in Brazil you would be mixing with much poorer people.

We went into one of the bars off the lane which turned out to be a good laugh. They were playing at full blast all these songs which had been adopted by Dutch football supporters. For instance, *We've Got The Whole World In Our Hands*. Plus "We love you Holland, we do", which sounded like it was sung by Papa Smurf, *We Are The Champions* from Queen, and Dutch versions of *You'll Never Walk Alone*, and *Always Look On The Bright Side Of Life*. We made sure they played a few England songs as well, including *World In Motion* and a laughable version of *God Save The Queen*.

After a few drinks at a couple of other bars, we made our way back to the Irish bar to watch a bit of Germany v Romania. The bar was too packed though so we just got the drinks in and sat around outside with about 50 others. A big cheer then comes out from the bar. "Germans must be 1-0 down" was the obvious conclusion. That wouldn't be good for us though. The result we would want from that game would be a draw.

Baggy and a few others had fallen asleep, probably due to lack of sleep rather than too much alcohol. We'd been drinking for nearly the whole day but none of us felt that pissed. Apparently the Dutch had lowered the alcohol to 2.5%. Probably a good idea.

After having a pretty decent buffet at a nearby Chinese restaurant it was time to make our way to the stadium which was only about a ten minute walk from the town square. We got there with about half an hour to spare before kick-off, had our tickets checked at the gate, then were let into the area around the stadium. Then as we walked on there was another barrier where we had to get our tickets checked for a second time. It was a big metal fence with a few narrow gateways. The ticket inspectors at the gate were taking their time letting people through and so the crowd started to build up and before you knew it you couldn't move.

We were all stood there waiting for about 15-20 minutes. We were all frustrated, but then a few people started pushing to try to create a surge forward. Which was totally stupid as there was a metal barrier in front of the crowd and kids caught up in the congestion. Everyone was shouting at the inspectors at the gate to just let us though, but they weren't listening. There was never a real possibility of anything serious happening, but the events of 11 years ago do go through your mind.

At the speed the queue was going we were also in danger of missing kick-off. I wouldn't put it passed the authorities either, as earlier in the season Arsenal fans were kept outside the stadium for the whole first half by riot police for the UEFA Cup semi-final in Lens. The Arsenal fans went mad and I don't blame them.

There was then another big surge forward from the crowd behind us, and this time it resulted in people just storming through the gateways. Talk about jobsworths - as this was happening there was still a man trying to inspect the tickets of people who were storming past him. He was quickly pulled away by one of his compatriots. What a tosser. Although the surge forward was stupid and dangerous, it did manage to get us all though. And once through everyone had a go at the ticket inspectors before making their way to the stadium entrance, where we had our tickets checked for the third time . . .

I was in the main England section behind the goal, while Jamie, Mel and Daz were in what was supposed to be the neutral section, but it was actually full of English - although Jamie did tell me afterwards that there was a load of Japanese businessmen sat behind them. Baggy and Ten were in the same part of the stadium as I was, but I lost them at the turnstile and couldn't find them afterwards.

The atmosphere before the game was absolutely brilliant. The England fans in my section were making so much noise and there was a real sense of optimism. Portugal had around 3,000 fans, but they were heavily outnumbered by around 20,000 Englishmen. The stadium itself was very smart and well designed. The only thing that let it down is the 30,000 capacity. The Dutch in the stadium were easy to pick out with their orange t-shirts. They seemed to be supporting England.

There was about 15 feet of standing room from the front row to the metal barriers near the touchline. As I was standing there this ape of a bodyguard comes storming through, shouting "Out the way, stand back." Then I saw Posh Spice walk past me. A few people then noticed her and started taking photos. She was very small and very average looking. Nobody would have noticed her if the bodyguard had not been a complete prick and brought her to people's attention. Knobhead.

The teams then came out onto the pitch and lined up for the national anthems. As usual, God Save The Queen was sung at a faster speed by the England support than the music that was being played. That always happens. While the national anthem that's being played over the tannoy system is still on the first verse, we're all on "Send her victorious . . . " Over enthusiasm. Nothing wrong with that.

As the match kicked off there were about 50 of us still stood up in the standing room between the front row and the metal barriers. Fucking brilliant, standing up at football once again, you can't beat it. The stewards then started asking us to get back into are seats. I obliged. Then Beckham puts in a beautiful cross which Scholes gets a head to. The ball hits the cross bar, then bounces up into the top of the net. Couldn't believe it. Three minutes gone and it was 1-0. Back down to the standing room to go absolutely mental! It was the nearest thing to being back on an open terrace again. No horrible plastic seats around me as I was celebrating, I was fucking loving it. It would be great if they brought back terracing to top flight football, but I know that it will never happen. I just hate all seater stadiums.

Even though we were 1-0 up, Portugal had all the possession and looked the more dangerous side. I have to admit that Seaman didn't look too confident and missed a couple of crosses that we nearly got punished for. He made up for it though with a great save from a long range effort from Costa. By this stage the stewards were just about getting us back up to our seats. Then Beckham puts in a beautiful cross (sounds familiar), McManaman's on the end of it and it's 2-0! Straight into the roof of the net. Time to go back to the standing room to go mental again.

I couldn't believe what was happening. We were all going mad. By the time a conga had started at the front, the stewards had decided they'd had enough and sent us all back up into the stand then blocked off the front of the aisle so we couldn't get back down again. I couldn't be arsed to find my seat so I just stood in the aisle with the rest of them.

The team were actually starting to play quite well. Some of our passing was starting to pay off, and I remember at that point thinking, "This is the best England game I've been to. It's never gone this right before."

News had gone around that the Germany - Romania game had ended 1-1. This started a chant of "We are top of the league, say we are top of the league!" Oh dear, talk about tempting fate. There was a man with a Southampton baseball cap joining in, which is probably the only time he's ever had the chance to sing that song, poor bastard.

It certainly did tempt fate, as not long afterwards Figo was given too much space and he blasted the ball into the England net from 30 yards. From where I was standing behind the goal it looked like Seaman could have done more, but after seeing it on the TV there was nothing he could have done. The whole atmosphere changed from then on. Before I knew it it was 2-2. Another great goal, this time a header from Pinto. The neutrals were getting their money's worth out of this game.

One thing that really wound me up was that the organisers played music over the top whenever a goal was scored. A lot of clubs in

England have started to do that as well. They should leave that sort of shit to the Americans. Fans are capable of celebrating a goal without some second rate pop song being played. It's a sad gimmick that totally cheapens the moment. Plus it winds up the fans who have just seen their team concede a goal. The music they were playing was UEFA's own official song for Euro 2000 so there was a bit of plugging going on there. Give me the sound of a crowd celebrating any day. UEFA can stick their song up their fat German arses. I don't attend football matches to listen to second rate pop music. If I wanted to do that then I'd watch *Top Of The Pops*.

During half-time I went for a walk round the stadium. There was no security stopping you going from one side of the stadium to the other. As I was walking around one of the stands, the announcer read out a marriage proposal from one of the fans in the ground. I looked up a few rows and saw a couple hugging each other and being applauded by everyone around them. She obviously said yes. Very nice.

I went back down to my section behind the goal for the second half. There was an uneasy feeling amongst the crowd as we'd been outplayed for much of the first half. That feeling was totally justified as well when Gomes made it 3-2 to Portugal in the 58th minute. I just turned away from the pitch and faced the floor. Couldn't fucking believe it. 2-0 up, 3-2 down. It had all been going so well.

From then on we expected an England onslaught. It never happened. The crowd gave some encouragement, but all we got was a gutless performance. Keegan, like Hoddle, can't seem to turn things around at half-time when the team aren't performing. The Portuguese ran the show. The only players to come out with any sort of credit were Scholes and Beckham. The Neville brothers were shit as expected. My mate, Lee, a fellow Gooner, summed it up when he said, "I wish they'd just fuck off and make a pop song."

In the few minutes that remained it was Portugal who had all the possession. Anyone would have thought they were 3-2 down. In the frustration, a man behind pulled down his flag from a barrier and somehow managed to elbow me in the head. I wasn't hurt or anything, but he couldn't apologise more.

Upon the final whistle a few players bothered to applaud the fans for their support. Most people applauded them back, whilst a few had a go at them. Nothing too strong though. I couldn't be arsed doing either, so just walked out and met up with Jamie, Mel, and Daz outside the ground. As we made our way back to the square everyone was under the same impression. We were gutless and beaten by the better team. No complaints.

There was no trouble either. Mind you, the main square was totally covered in litter so we'll probably get criticised for that instead. ENGLAND FANS TRASH EINDHOVEN, SHAMEFUL SCENES AS ENGLISH YOBS DROP LITTER, UEFA THREATEN BAN AFTER LATEST ENGLISH LITTER SHAME, LITTER THUGS. I felt sorry for the people who had to clean up the square though. You could hardly see the ground.

We soon made our way to the train station and headed back to Geldrop. The day had been typical of what we'd come to expect from following England. We'd had a good time off the pitch, but once again the football had let us down. There were a few Portuguese fans celebrating, but they weren't being provocative and didn't get any hassle. We had BBC back at the hotel so myself and Jamie watched a bit of *Match Of The Day* before Mark Lawrenson did our heads in with his post match analysis. We also watched a bit of the news in which it showed people watching the game back in England. As usual they showed scenes from the Sports Bar in London's West End. It's always the Sports Bar they choose to show pictures from whenever there's a big fight or an important football match. Is the Sports Bar full of the most genuine football fans in the country or full of trendy media types who only turn out for the big occasion? After all, it calls itself the Sports Bar yet has a no trainers door policy! I'm not quite sure how that works out.

We sat on the balcony for a while before crashing out. It was quiet outside apart from a bar full of locals who were still celebrating Holland's win over the Czech Republic. The first signs of life in Geldrop. For us the football had put us on a downer. We had the perfect tonic to make up for it though. Two days in Amsterdam, starting from tomorrow.

Day Four
Tuesday 13th June

(Jamie)

I WOKE UP feeling rough again, but felt better after some breakfast. Being sick before going to sleep seemed to have sorted me out a bit. It was funny, I could taste the crispy duck from the Chinese restaurant when it came back up. Best tasting puke I've ever had!

The weird thing I noticed as I stood looking out from the balcony of our hotel room, was that Geldrop finally had life! After two days of being a ghost town, a Sunday and a public holiday, there weren't just people on bikes and in cars and buses, but people everywhere. To carry on from Matt's observation, it's like the town had just woken up and come to life and people were suddenly put there just for our benefit, like on the film, *The Truman Show* (about someone who thinks he leads a normal life but finally realises that his whole world is a giant TV studio and his whole life is a TV series, and all events are based around him). Nice, modern little town, but very bizarre.

Anyway, after we checked out of the hotel we got the train to Eindhoven and then bought tickets for the train to Amsterdam. We'd all enjoyed our stay in Eindhoven and Geldrop, despite the result against Portugal. Eindhoven is a modern city, with about 20% of its working population employed by the electronics company, Philips, who also own the football team, PSV Eindhoven. It had been a good, laid back kind of atmosphere there, partly due to the attitude of the police and the fact that the local Turkish population in Eindhoven generally avoided the city centre whilst the English were there. Such a contrast to what we'd find in Brussels.

But first we had a couple of days in Amsterdam after which Mel and Daz would go home, so after a quiet train journey of about two hours, we arrived at Central station and went in search of accommodation. There was a hotel reservation service inside the station, so as Mel and Daz got some money from the bureau de change, me and Matt got a hotel sorted out. We got a place next to the Heineken brewery, about two miles away from the station, with four of us sharing a room.

After a taxi down there, we checked in and the owner showed us various places to go to on a map of the city centre. He pointed out an area just past the red light district which should be avoided after 1am, and Matt remembered that we'd stayed there two years earlier during the World Cup, when we'd had a break from France for a couple of days. The hotel owner just said it was full of dodgy smack heads and homeless people, but we'd be okay because there was four of us. He also pointed out where the best bars and coffee shops were, so after dumping our bags in our room and sitting about for half an hour, we headed off in the direction of the city centre. The weather in Amsterdam was very overcast and cloudy, unlike Eindhoven which was sunny all the time we were there (except at night surprisingly enough).

After walking for about a mile we got to Dam Square, which is where the main cathedral is and where the start of Damrak is, the main street leading up to Central station. Walking across there did my fucking head in, not so much the square itself but crossing the roads around it. It's not just a case of crossing the road when there's no cars or buses coming. No, in Amsterdam you're constantly looking left and right for bikes, cars, buses, trams, pigeons, none of whom give a toss about pedestrians. Even when the pedestrian crossing light is green for you to cross, cars still drive over them if they get the chance. The cyclists are complete psychos. How no one ever seems to get run over there I don't know, especially with the local delicacy sold in the numerous coffee shops.

It's made worse by the fact that most pavements are only a couple of yards wide, and even then there's usually obstacles in the middle of them forcing you to walk in the cycle lane. Still, after navigating our way across Dam Square and the roads around it, we went down a small shopping street, then getting bored of seeing endless shops, we went down a small alley leading to Damrak, stopping at a bar on the way.

The bar was okay, with only two other customers and some jazzy latino type music being played, but the barmaid was a bit of a fuckwit. She said it was her first day there, and had to phone someone (presumably upstairs) to work out how much four large Heinekens would be. A simple three second task on a calculator or cash till took a ten minute phone call for her. We were about to leave, but then she started pouring the beers. I got mine so I was happy, but after two beers the barrel ran out and she had to get someone from upstairs to change it. Finally, nearly 20 minutes after we'd arrived we all had a large Heineken in front of us. I have to say it was worth the wait because it tasted lovely. Just what was needed.

After that we headed up Damrak, then crossed over towards the red light district to see what bars were around there. There were loads of coffee shops with the smell of skunk and hash coming out of them, but none of us wanted to smoke any of that, we just wanted beer.

After a walk about we finally stopped at a bar opposite Central station, about 50 yards across a canal from Damrak. It was okay there, the four of us drinking away, having some chips and a toastie, watching the world go by. A Yank who was on his own at the table next to us started talking to us, and when I said we were over for the football and were gutted after the previous night, he replied "You'll have to excuse my soccer ignorance, what happened?".

I told him, then Mel asked where about in the States he was from. The Yank said, "New York, have you heard of it?"

Twat. I replied, "No, I've heard of York, in England, didn't know there was a new one though. Where is it?"

The conversation with him quickly died out and he went to pay his bill. Me and Daz making various references to Vietnam probably didn't help, but who gives a fuck. I don't mind Americans, and I'd rather we have closer economic and political ties with them than Europe, but the ones you find in Amsterdam are usually right wankers. And I'm sick of Hollywood rewriting history as in making a film about how they stole the German's Enigma code in World War Two, when the British had already captured it, and making films which portray the English as the evil Nazi-style invaders as in *The Patriot*. As if the British Empire was the world's only empire, and the Scots, Welsh and Irish had no part to play in it. And they seem to forget how they slaughtered and starved the native American Indians. In these politically correct days, it seems that even Hollywood realises that the only nation in the world you can still have a go at is England. Anyway, enough about Americans. After paying our bill we went off down by the canals in search of another bar.

It was only about 5pm, but there were already loads of dodgy looking fuckers around, mostly black, asking if we were English and called Charlie! They did my head in. It's difficult to resist telling them to fuck off. Why do they think we want charlie, ecstasy or hash just because we're English? They hang around at every bridge that goes over the canals in the red light district, just waiting for eye contact before coming out with the usual, "English? Charlie, ecstasy, hash?"

Most of them look totally wasted, and must live a sad fucking life. Anyway, after walking past a few of them irritating wankers, we found a bar with a few other English and sat outside for a while.

Slight problem, the beer tasted like shit. It had a funny after taste and we came to the conclusion that it was something like that funny Oranjeboom stuff. So we left the beer and went across the canal to another pub called The Old Sailor.

We were suspicious at the name to say the least, given the amount of poof pubs around, but it was full of English football fans and seemed okay. The beer was much better as well. Talking of poofs, I think I won the award for calling other people a poof the most, usually because they hadn't finished their drink and I wanted another one.

As we were sat there, and I was in the middle of saying something, I stopped in mid-sentence as some cunt wearing a Hartlepool scum shirt walked past with four or five others. Scum bastard. Put me off my beer for minute. But only a minute. I hate them wankers. But this was Euro 2000 and time to try to forget about such rivalries.

After another beer we went back to the other side of the canal into another bar, which had table football upstairs. After several mad games of that, my brother Dan phoned from Norway to say he might come down to Brussels at the weekend. He also mentioned he could maybe get tickets for the Romania game from someone there and would know the next day whether he could or not.

We went to another bar, this time in the opposite direction to Damrak, but finding the area a bit quiet apart from a group of tramps sat on a couple of sofas, we went back to the Old Sailor pub. By this time (early evening) it was fairly full in there, and the singing had already started, so we got our drinks in, found a table to stand at, and joined in with the singing. It was all the usual stuff - *No Surrender*, *God Save The Queen*, *Dambusters*, but it was good to be in Amsterdam and to have found a bar taken over by the English making loads of noise.

The barman in there put on a Madness CD, which had virtually the whole pub dancing and singing along, much to the bemusement of the tourists wandering about outside. He kept on stopping the CD and shouting, "Sing my song! I can't hear you . . . Who ate all the pies!" This was followed by everyone singing, "Who ate all the pies, who ate all the pies, you fat bastard, you fat bastard, you ate all the pies!" The barman loved it.

The singing of the England songs started again, and although there were a few police gathered about on the bridge over the canal outside, they were keeping away from the pub and weren't up to anything. The only thing they did do was tell the barman to close the windows, which had to be bolted down because we all kept opening them due to the heat in there. They wanted the windows shut mainly because of the noise, but probably also because one lad chucked a glass out the window at a Turkish looking lad who peered in, and someone else followed it up with an ashtray. Soon got rid of him.

It was a good laugh in there, drinking and singing, and talking to various people in there, such as Bury, Burnley and Oxford lads. One of the Dutch barmen made me laugh. Every time he picked up an empty glass, someone bought a drink, or anything else, he would say, "Cheers, mate," in an almost perfect Cockney accent. I think that was about the only English he spoke.

After a few hours in there we decided to go for a wander. We just ended up walking around aimlessly amongst the crowds, looking at what was on view in the windows. After another quick deink at the Old Sailor, the four of us decided to go for a curry, and found an Indian restaurant down a small alley, just off Damrak. Apart from us there was only one other group in there, about seven or eight English, and they left after a while. The poppadoms were shit, but I thought the curry (chicken Madras) was okay. Daz was absolutely fucked though, and kept falling asleep in between chucking rice all over the table. It was soon time to go, so we bought a bottle of water each, got a taxi back to the hotel and crashed out.

Day Five
Wednesday 14th June

(Matt)

UNFORTUNATELY, MEL AND Daz had decided to head back home to England a day early. It would be a shame to see them go, but the money had run out for Daz, and Mel didn't fancy the prospect of travelling home to England by himself the next day. When you're on holiday you often don't realise what you're spending and as for Daz, I think it was a case of too much beer harming the bank balance.

After a walk around the red light district, Mel and Daz made their way to the train station and headed off back to England. It was now down to two of us, me and Jamie. We spent the afternoon walking around the city and having a few drinks. We got talking to a couple of Swedish fans outside a bar who would be travelling to Eindhoven the next day for their match against Turkey. They had heard rumours that some English were staying behind in Eindhoven to help the Swedes fight the Turks, but I don't know how true that was. They followed English football and had been to Stamford Bridge to watch a match when they were last in London. They said the atmosphere was shit, and although I didn't want to stick up for Chelsea, I had to admit to them that no English ground has a decent atmosphere anymore.

Later on in the day we stopped off at a Waterstones bookshop and started to read a few of the English newspapers. I had a look at the tabloids, and surprise surprise, they was full of shit. One headline read 'Land Of Dope And Glory'. The 'paper was claiming that the reason there was no trouble in Eindhoven was because all the English were off their heads on dope. I quote, "England fans were too stoned to start trouble in Eindhoven, thugs who would normally be fighting were too high on hash to start throwing chairs around in the square". And, "Skinheads just shrugged as we lost to Portugal".

The article sounded like it had been written by a ten year old. For starters the whole piece was totally inaccurate. Yes, there were some spliffs going around, but most people were just drinking beer. I honestly didn't see that many people smoking hash. No more than your average England match where you always get some people who are skinning up. It was also claimed that England fans were too high to fight a mob of a thousand local Turks who were waiting for us at Eindhoven station. The Turks must have been invisible because we didn't see them.

Because there was no trouble off the pitch they decided to make a big deal about how England fans had been abusing Beckham after the Portugal game.   They made it sound like it was a large percentage of us when it turns out that there was a small group of about ten people giving him grief. It was such a small incident that none of us inside the stadium noticed it.   Beckham gets good support when he plays for England, yet they make out that we're all against him. The fans who did have a go at him were described as drunken yobs, so they obviously hadn't been on the hash that everyone else was supposed to be on!

It was also reported how England fans shouted out things like "Shame on you" and "You're a disgrace" when some of players came up to applaud us after the game. How can the press criticise us for that when that's what they put on the back pages every single time we fail to win a game? I wonder if they realise their hypocrisy, or whether they are just totally thick.

In the entertainment pages, I read a small article on how Keith Allen along with the rest of Fat Les, and Stephen Fry, had been on a five day bender that started at noon on a Friday. How incredibly interesting.   But then I thought to myself, wait a minute.   I was working as a walk on extra that Friday in a production involving Keith Allen and Stephen Fry. It went on until the early evening and they were both stone cold sober! There was a bar in the studios, but I never saw them in it. Just goes to show how full of shit the papers really are.

Anyway, enough of the press. We made our way down to the Heineken brewery to see if it was open to the public, but when we got there we found that it was closed, so we just went back to the hotel to pass out for a bit. I would have liked to have gone to the Van Gogh museum, but I don't think Jamie was too keen. I know it's not the sort of thing to do when following England abroad, but I saw a couple of Van Gogh paintings when I was in New York and he's one of the few artists that I like. The other main tourist attraction in Amsterdam was Anne Frank's house, but I'm sure it's no different to any other house in Amsterdam.   There were a lot of signposts pointing to Anne Frank's house, which I think is a little unfair if you've got legions of Nazis looking for you. It's no wonder they found her!

By the evening we made our way down to the red light district and to the Old Sailor pub that we'd been in the night before. The red light district was surprisingly quiet, as was most of Amsterdam, compared to what it had been like two years ago during the World Cup. We'd gone there for the weekend after the Columbia game in Lens, and the place was buzzing. We thought that Euro 2000 would be more of the same but it was very different. One thing that hadn't changed was all the dodgy drug dealers that hang around on every corner. Each time we passed them we knew what they were going to say. "English, charlie, ecstasy". It became fucking irritating but it was important not to give them eye contact.

In the Old Sailor we ended up talking to lads from places like Brighton, Luton, Blackpool and Birmingham. *The Sun* newspaper was being passed around and basically laughed at by everyone who read it. No-one could get through the first paragraphs without sitting up and saying, "That's bollocks". After a couple of hours, the pub was up and singing again like it was the night before. A few Madness tracks seemed to get people going. *Hey Jude* from The Beatles was also played and had the ending changed by the choir of St George to "Na na na na, na-na na na, na-na na, England!".

It was a good laugh in there and basically the whole night was spent drinking and singing England songs. Just what we were looking for really. Belgium were playing Italy on the TV, but nobody was really talking an interest in it. By about 1am we were both a little fucked so we decided to call it a night and make our way back to the hotel.

On our way back, we tried to find some decent places to get some food, but the only places that were open were kebab shops. We went into one in which the owner tried to rip me off, but I wasn't having any of it. He was a miserable twat as well, he didn't like us and he knew that we felt exactly the same way about him. As we left, Jamie said something about how he crapped on the cubicle floor in the bogs because there was no proper toilet. He was more than happy to let the owner know about it as well.

We'd been in Amsterdam for two days and neither of us had smoked one spliff. Just couldn't be bothered I suppose. Plus the fact that all those coffee shops are full of American grunge kids who are a pain in the arse and always seem to say things like, "You guys here for the weed? Alright yeah!" There's one strong argument for not legalising weed in England.

A lot of people go to Amsterdam purely for the drugs which in my book is pretty pointless as you can get drugs anywhere. I remember one dope head saying to me, "Yeah man, but it's not the same as having the freedom to sit in a public place and smoke a spliff." Fair enough, but is sitting in a dingy coffee shop all day smoking yourself to the point of dehydration really that much more of an adventure than doing the same thing in your living room in front of the TV? Anyone who's been into one of those coffee shops in Amsterdam will know what I mean as they're not the most exciting places on earth.

It's a nice city, but because of its liberal laws it attracts a bad mixture of irritating drugged up backpackers and the just plain sleazy. It's also so full of people from other countries (admittedly that's me included) that people who were born and brought up there must feel like a stranger in their own city. In a way it's like the centre of London in the sense that when you're in London you don't meet very many people who are actually from the city itself.

Oh well, we soon made our way back to the hotel and crashed out. It had been a decent couple of days in Amsterdam, but the next day we would be leaving our Dutch friends and making our way to Brussels. The Dutch hospitality was spot on, so we'd just have to wait and see how Belgium could handle things.

Day Six
Thursday 15th June

(Jamie)

I WOKE UP with the usual hangover, and after five days of drinking, smoking and singing, I had completely fucked my voice. I laughed my head off though when I remembered what I'd done the night before. "Oh yeah", I said to Matt, "I shit on the Turk's floor!"

Basically, when we went into the food place after the pub, I was bursting for a shit, so went to the toilet after ordering my food. The thing was, there was no seat on the toilet, so I had to squat over it. Us civilised Englishmen aren't used to such things, so my aim wasn't too good, especially with my deposit not being very solid having lived on beer for the last five days. The shit went all over the back of the toilet, but mostly on the floor, leaving a right fucking shitty mess. After I'd eaten my food, I said to the Turkish owner, "Oi mate, your food was alright, but you've got no seat on your bog so I shit on your floor," and walked out laughing. I shit on Turks!

Yet again I missed breakfast, so once we'd both packed our stuff we headed up to Central station to get the train down to Brussels. The weather was still overcast. It's funny how it can be dead sunny 50 miles away, but the weather is always shit in Amsterdam. But that didn't stop one bloke roller skating with almost nothing on! I was just walking along and Matt said, "He can't do that!" I looked over and saw someone flying along the road on a pair of roller skates, wearing nothing but a pair of swimming trunks and a small haversack. You get all sorts in Amsterdam!

After a quick stop for a drink of water, we were soon at the station and went to the ticket office. The place was full of American travellers and it took ages to get seen to in there. We had to queue to get a ticket to queue to get a ticket! In other words, you need a ticket with a number on it, and when it's your turn to be seen, your number appears on a digital display with the counter number you're to go to. After about half an hour I became worried that they wouldn't accept Visa, as a few places in Holland didn't and they only displayed a Mastercard sign on the door. So I went to the cash machine around the corner, returned five minutes later to find that Matt was being served and that they did accept Visa.

We got the tickets to Brussels, which were about £15 each, and after getting some food, we went to the platform to wait for the train which would leave just before 1pm. I wish trains in England were as cheap as in Holland. The journey from Amsterdam to Brussels would last about three hours, but we were paying only about £15. The same in England, say from Northallerton to London, would cost about £60. Rather than burden road users with ever increasing taxes, the government should provide incentives to use rail services and reduce prices to levels similar to those in Holland, through some sort of subsidy or some kind of private finance scheme with the new rail companies.

Once the train came I decided to pick a seat opposite a gorgeous blonde Dutch bird who had been waiting on the platform near us, just for a bit of extra scenery on the journey. She was a babe, but with my head being in the state it was, and my voice being as fucked as it was, I didn't bother talking to her. It was a fairly quiet journey, passing through Den Haag, Rotterdam, Antwerp and a few other places. Most people seemed to fall asleep at some point, and I think I managed about half an hour's kip too.

After three hours travelling we finally pulled into Brussels, where me and Matt got off the train. The platforms were all underground, so after climbing a couple of flights of steps, and then getting some money from the change place and a cash machine, we got a taxi from the station to our hotel.

We didn't have a clue where the hotel that I'd booked was in relation to the station, so getting a taxi was the best option. It turned out to be less than a mile away and was in a fairly central part of Brussels. Once we'd checked into the hotel we went to our room which was on the eighth floor. It was small and also had a fucking irritating pneumatic drill going on about 100 yards away. It was okay though, and after a shit, shower and shave, I got a phone call from Dan saying that he couldn't get a flight down from Norway for the weekend due to all flights to Brussels and Amsterdam being fully booked. The bloke with the Romania tickets had also sold them a week earlier. But then I got a phone call from the England Members Club saying that they had some cancellations for the Romania match and had a spare ticket for me, as I'd asked them before I left to phone me if any tickets came up. So although I've slagged off the FA about tickets in general, I have to say thanks for the phone call.

After being in the hotel for an hour and with the drilling still going on outside, it was time to go for a wander. Matt just wanted to get his bearings by walking about, but with me being there that would inevitably lead to stopping at various bars. Which is what we did. We walked around the block and soon found a bar, where I had three Stellas to Matt's one. The glasses held about two thirds of a pint and one beer cost about 70 pence, which is pretty cheap in my book. The beer tasted spot on as well.

From that bar we went back to near the hotel and headed in the general direction of the station where we'd come from, as that looked a more lively area. We were both hungry and both fancied an Italian meal, so on finding a street that was full of Italian restaurants, we went into the first one for some food. The food was nice and fairly cheap (we both had tomato soup followed by a pizza) so we decided we'd probably go back there another day.

Once we'd got our beer base for the evening we headed up towards the main square, La Grande Place. Just before there was a smaller square with a couple of bars with a few English sat outside, so we decided to have a few beers there. The general atmosphere about the place was quite relaxed, although there wasn't that many English around the city, with most likely to come out on the Friday before the Germany game at the weekend. We got talking to a couple of Stoke City lads who were sound enough, so we went on with them to find another bar that was showing the football, Sweden v Turkey. The first pub had a TV, but the staff were unable to tune it in to the football, so we left without getting a drink and found an Irish bar around the corner.

This one had a big screen with the football on, and the West Ham lads were there who'd been outside the bar in the square. When I got to the bar I asked for, "Une grande biere," and the barman replied "A point a what?" in a broad Irish accent. So I took the piss out of him when he said "A hundred tirty" (i.e. 130 BF).

The football was shit, ending 0-0, and we heard that it had kicked off after the match, but seeing as there were no English there, nothing was made of it in the media. We had a good laugh in that bar, talking to the two Stoke lads, a few of the West Ham lads, and a few others that were in there, including a couple of Arsenal fans. The beer was going down well and we had a good sing song, doing the usual thing and singing *No Surrender* in an Irish pub, with one of the West Ham lot waving his red hand of Ulster flag.

We went back to the hotel just before midnight, stopping for some food and water on the way. It had been a good night, and I crashed out within two minutes, although Matt said I attacked the chair at the end of the bed in my sleep, kicking it across the room and shouting something! Dunno what I was dreaming about.

Day Seven
Friday 16th June

(Matt)

FOR WHAT WAS to turn into a nightmare, all I can say was that the day started off well enough. We were in a Waterstones bookshop near the hotel and I was reading one of the newspapers when I noticed that standing next to me was a member of ITV's commentary team for Euro 2000. An ex Premier League football manager who's name I can't reveal.

He pointed to an article in one of the newspapers and said to me, "That's the best thing I've read this whole tournament." The article rated him as the best football pundit on TV for Euro 2000. So you've probably guessed that it wasn't Ron Atkinson I was talking to! He then asked me if we were going to today's match. He was referring to the France v Czech Republic match in Bruges which is about 60 miles from Brussels. I told him that we hadn't planned to.

He then offered me a couple of tickets. I asked him how much, but he was giving them away for nothing. Of course I said yes, so he then told us to come with him round the corner to the Sheraton Hotel where he was staying, where we could pick the tickets up. Couldn't believe it, we were going to get free tickets for a Euro 2000 match between two of the best teams in the tournament. And in Bruges as well, the nicest city in Belgium. I'll never slag off this particular football personality again. As we were sat in the reception, he came down and handed us the tickets.

All he asked from us was that we went to the game, and that we didn't sell them. If we did then that could get him into trouble. He said he'd rather give the tickets away to people who would watch the game than see them go to waste. What a result. He didn't have to do that for us, and it was much appreciated.

He had told us that it was a 5pm kick-off so we immediately made are way to the train station. The train to Bruges was mainly full of English fans, none of whom had tickets, but all were hoping to get some in the city centre or around the stadium.

We got to Bruges at about 1pm and headed straight for the city centre. Bruges is an old medieval city in the same way that York is. I'd been there before and was delighted to be back. The place was full of Czech Republic fans. I didn't think there'd be that many of

97

them, but they definitely outnumbered the French. The French turnout was quite disappointing considering they border Belgium and are World Champions. Unlike England, I don't think their fans travel unless they've got match tickets. I never saw one ticket tout the whole day.

The Czechs were all round the city centre and just drinking and singing their way through the day. They were a good laugh in fact, and we got talking to a few of them in the main square. They all followed English football and a couple of them were Arsenal fans. They loved the fact that we were English, which was nice as most Europeans can't stand us. Apart from maybe the Dutch and the Scandinavians.

They knew so much about English football that they'd even heard of Darlington! When Jamie tells foreigners that he supports an English Third Division team called Darlington, they just respond with a polite, "Oh, okay." But when he told this group of Czechs, they responded with "Ah yes, Dar-ling-ton. Same division as Roch-dale, and Hal-i-fax. Here's another one, Macc-as-field."

They went through the whole Third Division almost and then Cardiff which gave Jamie an opportunity to tell them about the scar on his forehead. They had some bet on at the start of the season which predicted the winners of all four English divisions, and Cardiff and Macclesfield had let them down in divisions Two and Three.

There were a few French fans in the square who were having a singing match with the Czechs. One Czech threw a glass of beer at them, but apart from that there was no trouble. If there was, then myself and Jamie would probably have been nicked for being English! Like the Portuguese in Eindhoven, the French and the Czech Republic fans looked like tourists. They were all kitted out with cameras, rucksacks and those bloody jester hats. Among the Czechs that we were talking to was a lad from Poland. Seeing as Poland didn't qualify he thought he'd still make an appearance and support his neighbours instead. Can't see that ever happening in Britain.

I wasn't in the drinking mood. We'd been drinking every day for the last week and I had decided that I could do with a day without alcohol. We made our way to the stadium via the special buses that were laid on at the train station. If you had a match ticket then you travelled for free.

It seemed to take forever to get to the stadium though. It was only three miles away from the station, but the driver took some fucked up route round the outskirts of the city and made the journey last between 30 and 40 minutes. It was boiling hot as well because whichever idiot designed the bus forgot to add opening windows.

The stadium was in a quiet residential area that was mostly full of pensioners. They were all sitting outside their houses looking happy and relaxed to have the tournament in their area. Some of them took advantage of it by selling food on their doorstep, which was probably better value than getting ripped of inside the stadium. Good luck to them. Like in Holland, you also see people of that age cycling in the street. I do remember at that point thinking that Belgium's not such a bad country and that it receives a bad press. I wouldn't be thinking that for long though.

Like in Eindhoven we had our tickets checked three times before entering the stadium. It had got to about ten to five and the stadium was only about 10% full. We thought that people must have had trouble getting to the stadium. I then looked at the match ticket which said, kick-off 18:00 hours. Bollocks. We'd got there an hour early. The football pundit that gave us the tickets must have got confused with the time in which ITV were scheduled to show the match live back in England.

By the time it reached kick-off the stadium had filled up. To give them credit, the French fans in the stadium got behind their team well and created an atmosphere that lasted the whole game. The Czechs got behind their team as well, but by the time they were 2-1 down they just looked pissed off. At one point I thought they were England in disguise. As the Mexican wave came round to their section they stayed in there seats and told the French to fuck off. This received jeers from the rest of the crowd, but myself and Jamie gave them a round of applause.

As the final whistle went we headed straight for the train station to get the train back to Brussels. It was a pretty decent game and both teams looked like they'd walk all over England if they were to play us.

I remember being bored on the train. I'd been on a lot of trains in the last week and was sick of sitting down on them with nothing to do. Funny how things change. Over the next couple of days I would be thinking, "I wish I was back on that nice comfortable train that was heading for Brussels."

Back in Brussels we headed for the city centre where the Grand Place was. There were police sirens going off everywhere and it sounded like it was kicking off. As we got closer, we found out that the riot police had blocked it off to all English football fans.

There was a nasty atmosphere hanging over the whole city

centre. As we walked down one of the lanes we saw a mob of about 30 local youths running up the hill laughing. They were a mixture of North African Arabs and Turks. It immediately reminded me of Marseille two years ago. The police just ignored them and ran past them and down the lane. As we got further down the lane and to one of the side roads off the Grand Place, we saw the riot police arresting a shit load of English outside a pub. It seemed like they were arresting anyone English that was there, whether they were troublemakers or not.

I couldn't believe how brutal they were either. The police were kicking and punching the English fans and hitting them with truncheons, then throwing them to the ground. There was no resistance from the English, but the police were still laying into them. They lined them all up on the floor, all handcuffed and in front of each other. I could see that image being on all the front pages the next day. I also saw a woman lying on the floor holding her head. Apparently she had been knocked over by the police.

Before I knew it, a riot policeman grabbed me and pushed me to the other side of the street while shouting, "Get over there." There were tons of tourists surrounding the area. They all seemed to be enjoying themselves, watching the free entertainment. The whole thing made me sick.

We decided to get out of there and find something to eat. As we walked back up the lane you could tell that there was a lot of English lads there who had come over purely for the fighting. There was one mob of about four who started laying into one lad simply because he was a Huddersfield fan. Kicking the shit out of him as he was on the floor until a couple of lads chased them off. It's wankers like that who should be arrested. But what did the police do? They went up and grabbed hold of the Huddersfield fan as he got back up. I didn't see what happened after that because we turned a corner, but as far as I know they arrested him.

We went down another lane where there were a number of Italian restaurants. At the top of the lane was a pub full of English who were singing. We went into the same restaurant that we'd been to the day before, and ordered a couple of pastas and tomato soups for starters. After what had gone on in the short time since we'd been back in Brussels I had a sick taste in my stomach. Immediately you could tell the difference between Belgium and Holland, and the way they handle things.

While in the restaurant we could hear it kicking off outside. The owners quickly brought in all the tables from outside and locked up.

There was a mob of Turks and Arabs at the bottom off the lane and they soon made a charge up towards the England fans in the pub. About 20 seconds later they all came running back down the hill again and past the restaurant. The English were charging them back down the hill and I went to the window to take a look. The few Turks who stood to fight were getting punched all over the place. Chairs and restaurant advertising boards were being thrown back down the hill. One big lad and a Turk were having a punch up as they were coming down the lane, before the Turk was sent flying off his feet with a knock out punch.

The big lad got nicked by two plain clothed officers who were quickly on the scene. As he was sat handcuffed a few yards from the restaurant, the Turk who was back on his feet went into the boot of a car and came out with a baseball bat. I don't know what the car was doing there as it was a pedestrianised area anyway. It might have been the car used by the plain clothed officers. As he went for the big lad who was on the floor, one of the officers stopped him, but just told him to calm down! It was very clear that the police were instructed not to arrest any local Turks or Arabs. Memories of Marseille. They were being handed an open invitation to riot.

The English had all moved back up the hill, and the area around the restaurant was becoming very dodgy with all the local youths hanging around. Jamie was wearing an England t-shirt and I had a baseball cap with the St George's cross on it so we would be obvious targets. Jamie suggested phoning for a taxi, but they wouldn't have come anywhere near the area. What worried me most was the thought of getting stabbed. You certainly couldn't rule out the possibility, bearing in mind what had happened in recent months. The local Turks were outside our restaurant and around all the back streets, and Turks are always tooled up.

After Jamie paid the bill on his Visa we decided the best thing to do was to get back up the lane and hang around by the bar where all the English were. Not too long after we got back up to the pub, the English were gathering together a mob to steam the Turks who were still waiting for them at the bottom of the lane. There was a war cry going on and you could see by people's faces and the conversation that they were out for revenge for what happened to the two Leeds fans in Istanbul.

The English then charged down the lane and went for them. One mad fucker was running down with a table umbrella. Most of us just hung around the pub and watched what was going on. It was difficult to see what was happening as it was all kicking off about

100-150 yards down the lane.

The whole holiday was then turned on its head. The last week had been a good laugh but things were about to change. Jamie went inside the pub to buy a beer while I was still stood outside. Less than a minute later I must have heard something and turned around. The riot police had come storming round the corner doing a full on baton charge. They were heading in my direction and had come round the corner so fast that I had no chance of getting out of the way.

That was it. I knew I was done for. I raised my hands in a way that was telling them that I wasn't involved, but I knew it wouldn't do any good. Incredibly the first two lines ran straight past me, but I was now surrounded by riot police so I knew that there was no escape.

One of them then started hitting me with a shield. I still had my hands raised, but then he grabbed me and threw me down front first onto the ground which was covered in broken glass. I seem to remember being kicked and hit with a truncheon as well. The second I got thrown to the ground all that went through my mind was that I was going to be deported and miss the Germany game along with the rest of the tournament. I couldn't believe what was going on. It was a nightmare come true.

It takes three of them to handcuff you. One to put their foot down on you (bare in mind I was on still lying on top of broken glass), one to kick you, and the other to tie your hands with those tight plastic cuffs. I remember telling them that I hadn't done anything, but it just seemed to wind them up even more. As I was lying on the floor, I looked round and saw Jamie still in the pub. At least he hadn't been arrested.

They then screamed at me and the other England fans in a similar predicament to get up, which is a little difficult when you're lying down with your hands tied behind your back. So when they see you're not moving they rough you up a bit. They picked us all up and then threw us back on the ground, where they sat us down with are legs apart and lined us up in front of each other. If they didn't think you were close enough to the person in front they kicked you into position. They were getting a real thrill out of their job. They were swearing at us in English. For instance when they hit us they would be saying things like, "You English wankers" or "Fuck you, fuck you." They hated us. One of them grabbed my baseball cap and chucked it on the floor. Fucking bastard. There were a lot of women coppers there as well who were just as vicious as the men.

And they call us barbarians.

They then moved us from one side of the street to the other. There was about five rows of us with roughly ten in each line. I still couldn't believe what was happening. I was even sitting among lads who weren't even English, but who like me were caught in the wrong place at the wrong time. One Swede who was behind me said to one of the coppers, "Why are you arresting me? I'm not even English, I'm Swedish."

The response he got was, "We hate the fucking Swedes too, you shut the fuck up," and the copper then booted him.

We then got taken one at a time down the lane by an officer. Again they would shout at us to get up, see that we couldn't do it, then rough us up a bit. To pick you up they would wedge their truncheons inbetween your arms and your back, and lift you like that.

The man who led me down the lane was a plain clothed officer who looked like Eddie Brimson, author of *Teargas And Ticket Touts*, and other such books. As we walked down he said this to me. "I am a Belgium hooligan, just like you. We hate the English, we hate the Dutch, we hate the Germans, we hate the Turks, we hate everyone. My team is Anderlecht, I am a Belgium skinhead, we like to fight too."

I told him that I wasn't a hooligan and that I'd done fuck all to be arrested, but he just replied, "Ah yes, but zero tolerance, you were unlucky."

At first he was quite rough, but once I got talking to him he completely eased the pressure on my arm.

Stood on the corner at the bottom of the lane were all the Turks who were being allowed to mock us as we were being led around the corner. They were all stood there laughing and applauding. You can imagine how much of a wind up that was. I feel about as much love for those people now as your average Greek Cypriot does. In fact I might join a few of my Greek Cypriot mates for the annual Turks Out Of Cyprus march that they hold each year in London.

I told the plain clothed officer that I had a ticket for the Germany match, and that I was gutted that I was now going to miss it. He assured me that I would see the game, as they were going to keep us for eight hours and then let us go. I couldn't believe that, but he promised me that that was going to be the case.

I cheered up all of a sudden. All I was concerned about was not being deported. If they were to let us go in the morning then I could handle that. We were then lined up on the pavement once again. There were two Canadian tourists in the line next to me who just couldn't believe what was happening to them.

A few of the policemen had taken their helmets off and by looking at them you could tell that they were Hitler's boys. Proper little Nazis. In the distance we could hear it starting to kick off again. It sounded like it was coming from near the Grand Place. The pigs then surrounded us with their batons raised. They must have thought we were going to get up and join in. Everyone just looked at each other as if to say, what the fuck are these lot on? We're sitting on the floor handcuffed and lined up in front of each other. Did the thick bastards honestly think that we were going to start kicking off? By the looks on their faces they did, which just goes to show how much they'd been brainwashed about us.

It was really uncomfortable sitting down with your arms tied behind your back. My back was killing me and my wrists were being cut up by the tight plastic cuffs. A smart dressed Turk in his late 30s walked right past us with his wife and started laughing and waving at us. A riot policeman then clobbered him with his shield and told him to get moving. The Turk and wife were kicking up a right dust about it as if they were treated unfairly. The piece of shit should count himself lucky that he didn't get arrested. What a hard man, mocking people who are handcuffed on the floor.

They then dragged us away and took us to a police bus. The officer who took me was trying to provoke me into putting up some resistance by digging his truncheon into my back, but I just totally relaxed myself and walked on. A lot of the people around me were normal looking lads who didn't look like trouble makers, especially the Swedes and the Canadians.

As I got on the bus a press photographer took my picture. I turned my head away, but I don't think it did much good. I wasn't worried though as I knew they wouldn't use my picture on the front page of any newspaper. They always use a skinhead with tattoos and a beer belly, so I knew I'd be alright.

On the bus they screamed at us to sit down and if you weren't quick enough, you were thrown into your seat. Once it got moving we couldn't see where they were driving us, as all the windows were blacked out. We were in there for a long time though and it seemed like they were going round in circles.

The two Swedes were sat two rows behind me and one of them started screaming in pain because his handcuffs were tied too tightly. There was no police in there with us so he had to take the pain. There were tears coming down his face and he was just shouting for someone to loosen his cuffs. A few lads who were blatantly trouble makers told him to shut the fuck up, which fucked me off because it was largely thanks to those stupid cunts that he was in that position in the first place.

We finally got to the detention centre and were left sitting on the bus for about an hour. The police came on to take one guy away who it turned out was a diabetic. It had taken them ages to come despite us shouting like mad for a doctor.

I don't know what provoked him, but one of the pigs grabbed the hair of the lad sitting behind me, pulled his head back and started beating him on the chest with a truncheon. Another pig who was on board saw what was happening and quickly rushed to join in. They then dragged him outside to give him a beating. A few minutes later he was sent back in to sit down. Understandably, he was shaken up by the experience.

The only human beings we were treated like were the ones from *Planet Of The Apes*. I'm not joking, that's what it reminded me of. The riot police were like the gorillas, only worse. One by one we were very slowly taken off the bus.   There were a couple of Norwegians lined up near the front of the queue, which upset one lad who told them that it should be English first. He was a mixed race guy with a beard and sounded exactly the same as Denzel from *Only Fools And Horses*. He was a West Ham fan from Liverpool and was a bit off a dodgy character.

As I got off the bus, the police took all my possessions and put them in a bag. They then gave me the bag and made me sign a form. The form was written in French, but I could just about make out that we were being held for disturbing the peace. I was then sat down on the floor with about 400 others. Our hands were still cuffed, but not behind our backs so it wasn't quite as uncomfortable. My hands had been cut slightly because of the broken glass back at the pub, but it was nothing serious.

A police van then drove up and aimed a water canon at us, just in case we were planning to disturb the peace again. The way we'd been treated so far we half expected them to use it on us as we sat on the ground.

Sitting around me were a mixed bunch, including a few Watford fans, a Pole from Warsaw, and a couple of Villa fans. One of the Villa lads was adamant that we were not going to be deported. He thought there was no way they could deport so many people. Loads of others shared his confidence and the general feeling was that we would be let out in the morning. I wanted to believe it, but couldn't see it happening.   When we were being taken to the detention centre, I was thinking back to when Chelsea fans were deported from Bruges not so long ago in similar circumstances. The Belgium authorities were not afraid of mass deportation.

I remember at the time Chelsea fans complaining about indiscriminate policing and that people were just dragged off the street and arrested for doing fuck all. At the time I thought they were probably telling the truth, but now I'm certain of it.

The Pole I was talking to was quite a decent bloke. Like most of us, he hadn't done anything to justify his arrest. He was a football fan though as he was wearing an Arsenal ring. I told him that once they found out that he wasn't English, they'd let him go. I hope I didn't raise his hopes too high.

Like many others, I was absolutely dying for a piss. So much so that it began to hurt. The temperature had also dropped which made the problem worse. Some people had been so desperate beforehand that they had taken a leak inside the coach, which needed other people's help bearing in mind our hands were cuffed behind our backs. Of course I asked the police if I could go, but as expected they didn't listen.

Eventually they started to move us all into this massive indoor horseyard which was about the size of a football pitch. The ground was a mixture of sawdust and manure. We were allowed to go for a piss by one of the walls, which by then was more needed than ever. It was hard though as my hands were tightly cuffed. As I was one of the first to be let in I was able to find a space by the wall (not the wall used as a urinal) which I could then lean against. We were not allowed to stand up and anyone who did was quickly told to sit down by some pig who looked like a bald Freddie Mercury. Fucking right nutter he was as well. I remember him smashing some lad against one of the walls.

Sitting next to me were a couple of Huddersfield fans who I recognised from Eindhoven. It turned out they live in Holland and that they had their car parked outside a hotel in Brussels. If they didn't get to it by nine in the morning then it would be towed away. They'd only been in Brussels about an hour and still only had Dutch guilders on them. I told them that I saw one of their fans get done over in Brussels by a group of English, but they didn't seem to mind because at least somebody hated them!

Overall there was somewhere between 300-400 of us inside the horseyard. Then one Turk walks in handcuffed. They'd actually arrested one of them! What the fuck had he done? Shot someone?

He was smiling and trying to act the tough guy, and a few lads got up and were gonna have a go at him. The police stopped them before Freddie Mercury took the Turk away and smashed him against the wall. This time Freddie was cheered. The Turk was then taken out of the horseyard.

At one point, everyone started whistling *The Great Escape* which actually brought a smile to the faces of some of the pigs. I had by now convinced myself that there was a chance that we could be let out in the morning. Only because of everyone else's confidence. A lot of them had probably been in this situation before and the general feeling was that there was too many people to send back home. I was praying that that would be the case. I could then take a taxi back to the hotel, pick up my match ticket and then meet up with Jamie.

One of the Huddersfield fans was worried that they could keep us for up to 30 hours because of new laws passed. Everyone else was under the impression that they had to charge us within 12 hours of arrest or let us go. Half of us were officially arrested at 10:30pm, the other half at 9pm. The morning couldn't come soon enough.

I was slightly concerned about how Jamie was going to get back to the hotel from the pub where I left him. It was under a ten minute walk, but he would have to pass a lot of Turks to get there. But as far as I knew though, he might've been arrested too and was being held elsewhere.

It had got really cold in the horseyard. There was no heating and all the windows near the top of the roof were wide open. And because it had been such a hot day we were all in short sleeve t-shirts. The horseyard was going to be our accommodation for the night whether we liked it or not, so all we could do was sit there and wait for the morning to come.

Some people managed to get some sleep in, but I didn't get any. I never got any sleep the night before either because it was too hot inside the hotel room and the bed was too small. The wall I was leaning against was uncomfortable which didn't help, but it was better than lying down in sawdust and horse crap.

Every now and then the officers would throw us bags of water to drink out of. They looked like they should have a goldfish swimming around inside them. The only way to open them was to rip the bag with your teeth then squeeze it for the water to come out, and try to drink it without spilling water all over yourself. Most of the bags thrown in ended up on the ground which made them undrinkable as you're not going to put your mouth on something that's covered in manure. My hands weren't much cleaner, smeared in dirt and the odd blood stain, and my wrists were totally fucked up and covered in red marks because of the cufflinks. I just hoped it would all be over come the morning.

(Jamie)

WHEN I LEFT Matt outside the bar to get a beer, I had no idea what was about to happen. There were probably about 20-30 people stood about outside the bar and the one next to it, with about a dozen inside the one I went into. I bought a beer, but the plastic glass was leaking, so I had to get another glass. Just as the barman was changing glasses I heard someone say behind me, "It's gonna go off again in a minute."

Once I'd got my beer I turned around to see a mob of riot police coming around the corner to the front of the bar, behind the lads stood out the front. Seeing this, I shouted out the open window to Matt, telling him to get the fuck inside. I don't think he heard me, but it was too late anyway because as soon as he turned around the riot police were right on him.

He held his hands up in innocence and a few of the coppers pushed past him, but then one of them went for him, knocked him to the ground, dragged him across the street and handcuffed him, adding a couple of kicks while he was lying there. The police had just gone in and battered anyone outside the bar, then arrested them.

I was fucking fuming, seeing my cousin and others being treated like shit, but there was fuck all I could do. A line of riot police faced the bar, batons at the ready, and a couple had tear gas canisters pointing at the bar. I thought they were going to come steaming into the pub and nick us lot as well, but when they did come in one copper pointed out someone stood at the bar and another one went in and grabbed him, dragged him outside, and gave him the same treatment as the others. One lad went outside, held his hands out and protested at the way everyone was being treated. Within seconds the riot police hit him and put him on the floor, cuffed him, kicked him, and dragged him across to the others who were being held. There was a crowd of press, tourists and locals having a good look at what was happening from around the corner, including a few jeering Turks, which was fucking annoying. Wankers.

Within ten minutes the police and all those arrested were gone. I didn't know what the fuck to do. I knew that Matt would probably be deported, but I would have to phone the British Embassy and Belgian police in the morning to find out for sure. I talked to a couple of Coventry fans who both bought me a beer, and they seemed quite understanding of my predicament, especially given the fact that I now had a half mile walk back to the hotel on my own wearing an England t-shirt, and I wasn't even 100% sure of the right way. It would've been dodgy enough with two of us making the journey, given the fact that the mob of Turks had been chased down that way half an hour earlier.

By 11.30pm, nearly an hour after Matt was arrested, and 20 minutes after a taxi driver refused to take me to the hotel because it was so near, I decided to walk it. I walked straight down the small street we'd come down earlier, got to the main street, turned right and headed straight along to the hotel. It took less than ten minutes, but for the whole walk I was looking at everyone, fists half clenched, looking behind me, walking towards groups of tourists and away from anyone who looked the slightest bit Turkish. I got back to the hotel without any hassle, phoned home to say what had happened, then watched *Match Of The Day* on BBC1, with Gerald Sinstadt saying that all those arrested would be deported. Fucking great.

A day that had started so well had suddenly become a complete nightmare. The police had been well out of order. Fair enough, they'd said they would have a zero tolerance policy towards any trouble, and they had to be seen to do something. But they were so fucking indiscriminate in the way they arrested anyone who even looked English. Meanwhile they did fuck all about the Turks who were having a go, most of them with various knives and weapons in full view. They just left them to laugh at those being arrested. Fucking Turkish scum. Fucking Belgian scum.

I'm not saying that everyone from those two nations is scum, but those in the centre of Brussels that night were (Belgian police, not ordinary Belgians). There was no need for the police to arrest everyone outside that bar. Okay, so some of those there may have been involved in minor scuffles with the Turks 20 minutes earlier while me and Matt were in the Italian restaurant. But that's no excuse for them to come marching around the corner, hitting, kicking, cuffing and arresting anyone in their way. All they had to do was make their presence known and separate the two groups.

But no, they were clearly given orders to nick and deport as many English as possible, which was clearly their tactic in Brussels for the whole weekend. Which left me on my own with two rucksacks for the rest of the trip.

Day Eight
Saturday 17th June

(Matt)

BY 6.30AM THEY had begun to take people out of the yard which raised hopes that they were starting to let people go free. Because they were taking people out at a very slow pace it would make sense, as they wouldn't want to release us all at the same time. 400 England fans all walking round the same part of Brussels looking for a taxi wouldn't be a good idea.

They were taking about ten people at a time and at a very slow pace. Each person was led away by two officers holding an arm each. As I was one of the first to be let into the horseyard I would be one of the last to leave it. At the time I thought I was unlucky.

One of the coppers decided to show he was human by offering to loosen handcuffs that were too tight. They had a struggle loosening mine and ended up using some nasty looking knife to cut through it. They weren't being too careful and at one point I thought they were going to cut my wrist. I asked them what was going to happen to us, and they told me that we were being kept for 12 hours, then they would decide what to do with us.

By 9.30am, there were only about ten of us left in the yard. We were all stood up and feeling restless as we didn't know what was in store for us at the other end. Two officers, one male, one female, then took me by each arm and started to walk me out. I was glad that something was finally happening. There was the anticipation that I could be set free and end up getting to Charleroi for the Germany game. There was also the worry that I was heading straight for the nearest airport. I was certain though that the worst part was over. As I walked out into the daylight I didn't know what was going to happen. All I knew was that I was glad to be out of that stinking horseyard.

As we left the yard, we were put in a small police van and taken to another building which was about half a minute's drive away. Once in the building they finally took our handcuffs off which felt great. To be able to move my arms about again was a fucking relief. They took us into a room where we had some mug shots taken, then we were sent through to a senior officer who was sitting down at a table. He gave me these papers, which I had to sign about two or three times. They were all written in French so I didn't know what I was putting my name to. As far as I was concerned I could be signing papers for my release.

They seemed quite interested in my surname. They found the name 'Bazell' unusual, which is odd because when I traced my name back, the only place I could find it was in the surname dictionaries of France and Belgium! It's a name that comes from the Huguenots who settled in Britain hundreds of years ago. I told them that to try to get me on their good side, but it didn't work. Credit to them, they knew what I really thought of them. At least they pronounced it properly. Baz-ell. Everyone in England gets it wrong and pronounces it Bazil. Although the fact they can say my surname properly doesn't hide the fact that they are the filthiest scum on the face of this planet.

The man sitting down on the table then emptied the see-through bag that had my possessions in it, and started rummaging around. He picked up my France v Czech Republic ticket and started to look at it. He looked really surprised, then asked me if I was English. When I told him that I was and that I went to the match, he turned to his other officers in confusion. He said something to the effect of "You are English, and you go to watch a match with France?"

He was both confused and impressed. How could a hooligan anglais be interested in a football match between two other countries? Just sums up the way they thought about us.

One of the pigs then asked me to take out my shoe laces and remove the belt from my jeans. I then realised that they were going to send me to a cell. They wanted to take away anything that could be used as a way of taking my own life. For fuck's sake, I was amongst some hard looking bastards. If I wanted to commit suicide all I had to do was call one of them queer. After I was searched they put a sticker on my t-shirt and I became number 57.

They then took away our bags with our possessions and took us through to the prison. There were four cells in the same block, two small cells at the front that were parallel to each other, and two larger cells at the back similarly arranged. In between them was a narrow aisle. One of the cells at the back was packed full of about 50 lads whilst the same cell opposite had just three lads sitting in it! One of them had tears in his eyes.

They decided to put us in the cell with 50 lads in it. As they did, I heard one of the three lads say, "Shit, we are in trouble." The one who had the tears looked even more distraught when he saw us walk into the cage of 50. They knew they were being singled out.

I can't say we were too thrilled about it either. Over 50 of us crammed like sardines into this little cell. The two smaller cells at the front were also full of people, but at least they all had enough room to sit down. All we could do was stand up. There were benches round the side so some lads were lucky enough to sit down and a few were sat on the floor, but there wasn't even enough room for us all to do that. Plus the floor was wet and dirty anyway.

There was the odd rumour going around that they were going to keep us in there for two hours. I couldn't stand the thought of that. Two hours sounded like an eternity, especially for those of us who can get claustrophobic. Although I don't think anyone could not be claustrophobic when they're in conditions such as these. I knew I wouldn't be able to take it. I don't get claustrophobic when surrounded by fans on a football terrace because you're always moving and there's something happening on the pitch that takes your interest. But here all we could do was stand still while not knowing what was going to happen to us. This was becoming a new nightmare. I'd rather have been back in the yard.

There was a growing feeling that we were going to get deported. Problem was there was no-one around to give us any information. The only officer to walk down the aisle and speak to us was some 18 year old who knew nothing about anything. All he could do was tell us that he was a junior officer and that he didn't know what was going to happen to us.

The only other pigs to turn up were officers who couldn't speak English and who fed us by chucking over these packaged waffles and more of those stupid bags of water. It was like watching sea lions get fed at the zoo. Everyone was complaining about the waffles and asked for some proper food, but we were just ignored. Personally they could have handed me a three course meal and I wouldn't have touched it. I had such a sick feeling in my stomach that I couldn't eat. There were no washing facilities either so I wouldn't want to touch food with my hands bearing in mind I'd spent the night in that horseyard. There was a tiny concrete room with a metal bog but it had no seat, no flush, no sink, and no light bulb. I knew when we came out to Euro 2000 that we would have to settle for cheap accommodation, but this was ridiculous.

We had been detained for over 12 hours and we wanted to know what the fuck was going on. Someone in one of the cells at the front had heard that we were going to be taken to the ferry port at Ostend and taken on a boat back to Dover. I needed to make a phone call to Jamie to let him know what was happening. Although I never gave up hope, I knew deep down that there was no way I was going to get to Charleroi to watch the Germany match. My ticket was in my rucksack back at the hotel and I wasn't sure that Jamie knew where it was. If I wasn't going to go to the match I could at least get some money out of it.

I asked for a phone call, but was told that I wasn't entitled to one. What? Surely that's the first right of any prisoner? Problem was when I asked them I knew they weren't going to let me make one. They knew they could treat us like shit because they could get away with it. They could do what they wanted and they knew it. Who was going to protect us? The British Government? The media? The FA? No fucking chance. They'd all be too busy condemning the violence to worry about the fact that hundreds of British citizens had been wrongly arrested in a foreign country and were being treated like the scum of the earth.

It just adds to the resentment. We were being treated with less rights than murderers and rapists. I also felt resentment towards some of the people I was sharing a cell with. What kind off fucking idiot must it take to come over to Belgium to start trouble? Didn't they see it on the news before they came over to Belgium? It was clear what was going to happen to people who were kicking off. The Belgian police were well up for it, and the people who were kicking off just played right into their hands. I've got no problem with self defence. I don't believe you should have to run if you think you can handle yourself, but the fact was that there were some English who came over purely for the fighting, and I wish the fuckers would just have stayed at home.

But that is still no excuse for the Belgian police to go about things the way they did. From my own experience of talking to people around me, I would say that at least half were innocent. Most of them had been in a bar off the main square that was CS gassed by the pigs. There were some known hooligans who had taken refuge in there, but the pigs gassed the bar and nicked 150 people. All of them said that the CS gas was one of the worst things they've ever experienced. Sounded like they had it worse than I did.

The people who were kicking off openly admitted that they did get involved. Some of them were proper dodgy characters who were in Brussels just for the ruck. Others were just normal lads who got stupid and carried away. Some of them looked as young as 18. Apart from a few exceptions, I was definitely not among a group of hardcore hooligans.

Sitting down on one of the benches was a middle aged man with glasses and a side parted haircut. He was wearing a tucked in smart shirt, with white trousers. Next to him was his son who looked to be in his early twenties. He too was quite smartly dressed, but had three boot marks in-printed on his shirt courtesy of the riot police. The fact that these two guys had been arrested really took the piss. The poor bastards, I don't even think they were in Brussels for the football. They looked about as thuggish as Hugh Grant. Their arrests underlined how bad the policing was that night. They both seemed very calm though. They were handling the situation better than I was.

If what happened to them was unfortunate, spare a thought for the Swiss bloke who was standing next to me. He was over in Brussels because he had won a competition to go to Euro 2000! Congratulations, sir, your prize is a good kicking by the Belgian police, one night's accommodation in a pile of horse shit, and a look around one of Belgium's prisons. Enjoy your holiday!

The hours passed by without any information. Just standing still amongst so many people got me more anxious with every minute that went by. I know it sounds trivial, but the fact that I had no shoe laces and no belt for my jeans felt really uncomfortable and made me feel even more insecure. It was also hot inside the cell and there was no air conditioning.

A senior officer then turned up and he eventually told us that we were probably going to be deported some time in the afternoon. He didn't seem to be too sure what was going on. He told us that the problem was that there are two police forces in Brussels, his lot, the Brussels City Police, and the scum that arrested us, the Brussels State Police. That's why they were having trouble sorting things out. We couldn't get any answers out of him because all he would say was that he was not making the decisions, and that it was all down to the Belgian government.

We then asked him about our luggage which was still back at our hotels. We were told that we would have to sort it out with the hotel once we were back in England. Then arrange delivery from a firm like DHL. I knew they wouldn't let us collect our bags. I remember during France 98 a load of French riot police stormed onto our train because a few lads didn't have valid train tickets. As they were dragging one guy away, he pleaded with them to let him pick up his rucksack that was still in the carriage, but they didn't listen and let the train pull away with his luggage still on board.

It wasn't so much a problem for me, because as long as Jamie was not arrested he would be able to look after my rucksack and then bring it home to England. A few people had the idea of arranging a taxi to pick the luggage up from their hotels, then bring it back to the detention centre. It was a good idea, but for some reason the police said that it would not be allowed to happen. Like myself, a lot of them had their passports, bank cards and other valuables back at the hotel along with their luggage.

The West Ham fan who sounded like Denzel asked to see the British consul, but he wasn't being listened to by any of the officers. I also heard him mention that he doesn't know how much longer his wife was going to put up with him getting into this sort of trouble. I think he might have had a couple of kids as well which added to his guilt.

We didn't actually believe that they had any idea what was going on. All they could tell us was that they thought we would be getting deported. We had been in the cell over four hours when we finally convinced them to move people out of our cell and into the one opposite with the three lads in it. About 20 from our cell were moved which left around 30 of us. At first it was quite a relief to have a bit more room, but the relief didn't last for long because the cell was still far too small to hold that number of people. We still could not all sit down at one time and the feeling of claustrophobia was just as bad as it was before. Even when I did get the chance to sit down I was up on my feet again in no time due to the anxiety. It was impossible to relax, and I couldn't stay still for more than a couple of minutes at a time.

There was one guy who had a medical problem and he kept on being taken away by the officers to a doctor so he could take his medication. He was quite a nervous person and had trouble communicating with people in a confident manner. There was no way on earth that this guy could have been a hooligan. Why couldn't the authorities have made a few obvious exceptions and let people like that go free? There were many people who it was obvious weren't hooligans just by looking at them. Maybe I didn't fall into that category, but I wouldn't have complained if those people were set free.

I noticed that in the cell opposite there was a lad with a broken arm. He had his arm in a sling and I think he might have been the one who got smashed against the wall in the horseyard by the bald Freddie Mercury policeman. Also in his cell were a few lads who were trying to find out some information about their mate who had been injured the night before. From what I understood, he was done over by the pigs.

At least half of us that were being held were by ourselves and had no friends with us. I think it must have been easier for the ones who were with their mates, as at least they had someone with them who they could trust. The rest of us were all strangers to each other, and it's amazing how lonely it can be packed in a cell with 30 other people.

In the cell opposite were the Huddersfield fans who I was talking to in the horseyard. They were trying to get the senior officer to understand that deporting them to England was no good because they lived in Holland. They had to be at work on Monday morning, and their passports were in their car that was parked in Brussels. If they were to be deported to England then they were completely fucked.

I couldn't help thinking back to the night before when I was arrested. If only we had stayed inside that Italian restaurant a few minutes longer then I wouldn't be in this situation. If I had gone inside the bar to buy a drink then I wouldn't have been surrounded by the pigs when they came charging round the corner. What stayed in my mind the most was being stood in front of the policeman who started hitting me with the riot shield before he nicked me. I tried to think of ways I could have got out of it, but there wasn't one. Once the pigs came charging round the corner that was it, there was no way out.

Looking back I can't believe I wasn't seriously injured. I was thrown on top of broken glass then stamped on, but it was only my hands that were cut. If I was wearing a thinner t-shirt then it probably would have been a different story. I had a tiny bit of glass stuck in one of my fingers which I finally pulled out that afternoon. It had felt like there was something there, but I couldn't see it at first because there was a small bit of blood that covered it.

The day just went on and on without any real information being given to us about what was happening. They kept on sending in the junior officer but he didn't know what was going on either. To be fair to him he had to put up with everyone's questions, and at least he was trying to make some effort to explain to us what was happening. A lot of lads did not make things easy by talking in a way that no foreigner who speaks limited English could ever understand. For instance, "'Ere mate, it's starting to take piss now, when the fuck are we gonna get some proper fucking food instead of those shite waffles?"

People with mobile phones were allowed to leave the cell and make a phone call, but only a few people actually had a phone on them. I offered money to one guy to use his mobile, but he had a pay as you go and didn't have enough call time on it.

By late afternoon the senior officer came in and told us that we were being deported by planes that were departing every half an hour from 6.00pm. Each plane was able to hold 80 people. It sounded like at the worst we should be home by Saturday evening. I was praying that I would be on one of the first planes out. I couldn't stand being in this cell for a minute longer, but I had that feeling that I wouldn't be one of the lucky ones.

Now that Jamie was all by himself in Brussels, I knew that he wouldn't want to stay there. I heard him mention that Baggy and his mates were staying in Lille until England got knocked out of the tournament, so I figured that he would meet up with them and go and stay in their hotel after the Germany game. My luggage was all together apart from my jacket which I hung up in the wardrobe. If I could get back to England in time then I could let Jamie know it was there before he left the hotel. It was a new jacket which I really didn't want to lose.

The senior officer then said that he was going to move people up to some of the cells upstairs which were bigger and had more air in them. Eventually we would all move up there. That sounded a lot better. He then read out some names who would then be transferred. All the names were people who were in the two smaller cells in the front. The only person from our cell to be moved was the bloke with the medical problem. The senior officer then promptly fucked off and didn't come back. At least 30 of us were just kept in the same cell in the same conditions as before. It was like being in a Third World prison. *Midnight Express.*

It was one of those times as well that I'm glad that I'm not a smoker. The craving for a cigarette amongst some people was immense. They needed one more than ever. Some of them had cigarettes in the plastic bags which housed their possessions, and which were lined up outside one of the smaller cells at the front.

When one lad went out to make a phone call on his mobile he went into one of the bags when the pigs weren't looking and was able to smuggle a packet of Benson & Hedges back into the cell. So much relief amongst the smokers once they were finally able to get that nicotine down their throats. Then not long afterwards, the craving would start up again. Jamie's become a bit of a chain smoker, so God knows what he would have done if he was inside.

The time was approaching kick-off for England v Germany. Deep down I always knew that I was not going to get out to see the game, but once all hope had gone it was very hard to take. I couldn't contemplate the fact that I was in a prison cell when I should have been in the stadium watching the game. I was feeling very sorry for myself. The fact that I was innocent made it even harder to take.

It didn't look like anyone was getting flown home either. No one from our four cells was being taken away so it was time to ontemplate the fact that we might be spending another night in custody. Some people were beginning to wonder if they were actually going to deport us at all. The officers never seemed too certain about it and there was a feeling going around that they had no plans to deport us and that we were going to be kept overnight and let free in the morning when tensions had cooled down after the England v Germany match.

That would have been much easier for all concerned as most people were scheduled to go home in the morning anyway. They could have let us all free after the match itself and there wouldn't have been any trouble. The way we'd been treated, not one person who was kicking off the night before would have got involved in anything after this experience. They would have just gone quietly back to their hotels and gone to bed.

A lot of people were saying how this was the last time they would ever go abroad to watch football again. Club or country. It's all become too much. I was feeling the same way. Authorities could only get away with this sort of treatment with English football fans.

I was standing by the door when I looked round and noticed that right next to me, in one of the smaller cells, was one of the West Ham fans who me and Jamie had been with on the Thursday night in Brussels. I hardly knew him at all, but it was nice to see some sort of familiar face. He was a skinhead, but he didn't seem like the sort of guy who would get involved in trouble. I knocked on the cage to get his attention, then started talking to him. On Thursday he was quite a cheerful person, but here he was just totally down, and I could hardly get a word out of him. He said he got arrested for doing fuck all, and was totally disillusioned about the whole business of following England abroad.

He just wrapped himself in one of the blankets provided and tried to get some sleep. I have to say that I was not really in a talking mood either. I found some space on the floor where a blanket was laid down and tried to get some sleep myself. I couldn't fall asleep, but I needed to lie down anyway just to calm myself down. Due to the anxiety I had been pacing up and down like a caged animal in a zoo.

People were wanting to know the score in the match, so someone suggested that we call for the senior officer to go and find out for us. A Sunderland fan made me laugh when he said, "Don't ask him. He doesn't know what the fuck's going on. He'll just lie to make us feel better. Fucking 10-0 with that bastard Shearer scoring a hat-trick.!"

After a while news somehow filtered though that it was 1-0 to England and the game was over. Shearer had scored the winner. There were a few half hearted cheers. It lifted spirits, but not by much. In fact nobody looked like they really gave a fuck. I certainly didn't. When your freedom gets taken away football doesn't really matter. I was glad we won, but I couldn't help thinking that there would be celebrations going on all over Belgium and England, and yet I was in a prison cell having the worst time of my life.

As the night wore on everyone was either sat on the benches or laid out on the floor trying to get some sleep. You could hear more England fans being brought through to the detention centre. They were singing so at least they sounded cheerful. I was half expecting Jamie to be one of them. A few of the lads in the cells looked just like Jamie and at times I thought it was actually him, and that he'd been arrested. I could have done with the company, but it was vital that he stayed clear of being nicked.

As it was coming up to midnight, people were starting to fall asleep. Me and a few others were being kept awake by one lad who was snoring like a fog horn. He was one of the lads who looked like Jamie so it was quite fitting that he should snore like him and keep me awake. I was beating it though and was finally on the way to getting some much needed rest. The senior officer then comes down the aisle and shouts to us all, "Okay, you will all be going home now, we have a boat scheduled to take you back to England."

Everyone then cheered and got up in anticipation. That was the last we saw of that senior officer. We waited and waited, but nothing happened. A couple of hours went by and no one came to take us away. For some reason he had decided to play a cruel joke on us. It must be that wonderful Belgian sense of humour that they're so famous around the world for. Why did he do it? Other than spite, there was no reason.

We will probably never have the chance to get revenge on that bastard or any of his Neanderthal colleagues, but I take some comfort from the fact that they all live in the dump that is Belgium which is punishment in itself.

Most people found it hard to get back to sleep after that. The temperature had dropped and it had become quite cold. Because the floor was wet, a lot of the blankets were damp so they were no longer much good. In the middle of the night I found a space on one of the benches and crawled up on it and somehow managed to get some sleep.

To say it had been a horrible day would be an understatement. I thought that once we were out of the horseyard the worst part was over, but I was wrong. By the morning I wanted something to happen, because one thing I did know was that I couldn't take much more.

(Jamie)

I WOKE UP without a hangover, seeing as I'd drunk less beer on Friday than any other day since leaving England. This was the big day, England versus Germany, but I was fucking pissed off about what had happened and couldn't really think much about the match at first.

I phoned the British Embassy, where an answering machine gave me the number of the British Consulate for Euro 2000. I told them what had happened, and the woman explained that there had been several hundred arrests, but they didn't yet have lists of those being detained or details of what would happen to them, although early indications were that they'd all be deported. I have to say she was quite helpful, and took Matt's name, my name and phone number, and said she would contact me if she could find anything out, but she thought I'd be more likely to hear from Matt when he got back to England before they heard anything.

I also phoned the Brussels City police and the Brussels State police, both of whom were arrogant, cocky and useless, so I ended both conversations by calling them twats. Belgian pig bastard scum. I decided that if I didn't hear from Matt, I'd assume that he'd be deported, and I'd leave Brussels the next day if I could find Baggy and the others who were staying near Lille, just over the border in France. I didn't know at the time that he'd got his phone to work abroad since being in Eindhoven, so I hoped he'd call me or I'd see him in Charleroi.

I got pissed off at waiting around and the sound of the drilling outside, so after midday I decided I had to get outside and go for a beer. There was a bar next to the hotel with a few other English sat outside, so I bought a large beer and sat next to a few Donny lads who were staying at our hotel. I started talking to them about the

120

previous night, but other than saying that those arrested would probably be deported, they weren't very talkative. I got talking to a couple of other lads about what had happened, and they seemed okay. After talking to them for a while, I asked them where they were from. Couldn't believe the reply.

"Hartlepool," one said.

"Fucking hell", I thought. "Fucking monkey hangers." I shook my head and laughed.

"Where are you from like?" one asked.

"Northallerton, and I support Darlington," I replied.

To my surprise they were okay with me, and we just talked about various incidents and matches between the two clubs. One of them was a Sunderland fan, but I had a funny feeling that I'd seen the other wanker somewhere. I know it's against my religion (Darlington FC), and I hate the scum from Hartlepool, but the morning after Matt was nicked I felt so fucking low, and these two were being okay with me, so I ended up going for another beer with them before going to the station for the train to Charleroi at about 3pm. I made a point of losing the two monkey hangers, partly out of principal and partly because I felt I'd end up doing something daft in revenge for what had happened after the England v Belgium game.

I saw Sven, Jon and the others at the station. They'd just arrived and were looking for accommodation. I told them what had happened and said to phone me if they got sorted and came down to Charleroi. The train was fairly full of English, and I talked to a Macclesfield fan and someone from Batley, West Yorkshire on the way down. The one from Batley said everyone from Keighley (where Baggy and a few of the others are from) is a complete nutcase, which I made a point of telling the others later.

There were loads of riot police at the station, stopping us from using one of the exits, and I heard someone say that it had gone off with the Germans in the main square in the morning. I followed the crowd over the bridge and went into the first bar for a beer. After that, I went to another bar, outside which a crowd of lads had gathered around some local bird, singing "Tits out for the En-ger-land!" to which she duly obliged.

I walked on for a bit and stopped at another bar, by which time I was feeling like Billy No Mates, although it was really Billy Cousin Deported. I talked to a West Ham fan for a bit, then stayed inside another bar talking to various Southerners. The match, like all of England's group games, was an 8.45pm kick-off, so at about 7.30pm I wandered up in the direction of the stadium, still not having heard from Baggy.

I was surprised at how few Germans were about, but the crowd was being well segregated and they were apparently gathered in a square on the other side of town. Once up at the stadium I went straight through the ticket controls and to the area just outside the stadium. I'd seen a few pictures of the stadium, and the big three tier stand looked as dodgy as fuck. It was at a very steep angle (37 degrees I think I heard somewhere), and the top tier was only temporary and would be demolished after Euro 2000. Still, I was in the stand behind the goal with the majority of people who'd got tickets from the England Members Club, and after going through a third ticket check I went to find my seat, right down the front of the stand.

When I got to my seat I realised what a crap view it was, with a great big fence and a yellow gate right in front of me. I was just glad to be there though, while Matt was still locked up somewhere in Brussels, awaiting probable deportation. He should have been in the stadium, enjoying the match, but no, the twat Belgian authorities thought otherwise.

As I looked around the stadium, it became obvious that England had taken the place over. We had all of the stand I was in, most of the main stand with three tiers (although there were a few Germans and neutrals in there), and a good section of the stand with all the media and executive boxes in. Only at the opposite end was it all German. There were England flags everywhere (except the German's end), although I'd left mine back in the hotel.

The teams came out and the national anthems were played, first the German one which was booed by two thirds of the crowd, then *God Save The Queen* which was sung as passionately as ever by the same two thirds of the crowd. Then it was time for kick-off. At last, our chance to beat the Germans for the first time in 34 years. At least this one wouldn't go to penalties. COME ON ENGLAND!

Once the match was underway both teams created a few chances, but England looked the better side and things were looking promising. As for the atmosphere, England won that one easily. *The Great Escape* was constantly being sung, along with all the usual England songs, but nothing can compare to the sight and sound of some 15-20,000 people around the ground, arms out to the sides, singing the *Dambusters* theme. Fucking brilliant! All we got in response from the Germans was the odd chant of "Deutschland! Deutschland!"

The first half ended 0-0 and I decided to go for a drink. As I was walking up the steps I heard someone shouting my name and then saw Baggy and Sour, who'd come back out with Northern Holidays having gone home after the Portugal match in Eindhoven. It was good to see them again after the day I'd had, and I told them all about what had happened to Matt in Brussels. Baggy said his phone now worked abroad, and that I should phone him the next day and go down to Lille and crash at their hotel. There were about 100 of them in two buses, all part of an organised tour, staying at the same hotel in Roubaix, just outside Lille, until after the Romania game on the following Tuesday. At least then I wouldn't be on my own in the shitty Turk infested Belgian police state EC capital, otherwise known as Brussels.

After getting a drink of water I stood next to Baggy and Sour for the second half. Obviously it was an all seater stadium, but everyone was stood up in our end and I was just stood in the aisle. It was certainly a much better view up there, about three quarters of the way up the lower tier, and with no big fuck off fence right in front of me.

The second half soon started, and within ten minutes England were in front. The ball was crossed in by David Beckham from the right, bounced over a group of players and fell just right for Alan Shearer to head in at the far post.

Yeeeeeaaaaaasss! We went fucking mental! All around me it was pure jubilation, although at the same time as jumping all over the place and going mental, I was trying not to fall over the crappy excuse for seats.

The rest of the match is a bit of a blur, although I seemed to be doing the wanker sign all too often, meaning Germany had missed yet another chance to equalise. The singing was almost non-stop once we were 1-0 up, especially with *Dambusters* and then *The Great Escape* which went on forever.

After losing our first game against Portugal, we could have been knocked out against Germany, but now at 1-0 it was a case of singing "We're not going home, we're not going home, we're not going, we're not going, we're not going home . . . Send the Germans home, send the Germans home, send the Germans, send the Germans, send the Germans home!"

We were fucking loving it! After a few missed chances from both sides the ref blew the final whistle and it was all over. "They think it's all over . . . it is now!" At last! We'd beaten the Germans. You'd think we'd just won the Cup we were that elated.

On the way out of the stand we were in, the three of us passed a line of half a dozen stewards and shook hands with every single one of them, us three grinning like mad and the stewards just looking totally bemused.

Once out of the stadium we went to the fountain on the big roundabout, where Baggy and Sour had arranged to meet the others before going off for their bus back to Roubaix. They soon turned up, and I phoned my brother Barney back at home, but couldn't really speak to him because of all the noise we were making - "Yeesss . . . Come On . . . Let's go fucking mental, let's go fucking mental, na-na na na, na-na na na . . . En-ger-land, En-ger-land, En-ger-land!"

Everyone all around was just so happy. Whether we won Euro 2000 or completely cocked it up, we'd beaten the Germans and that was all that mattered. Baggy said he'd phone me in the morning to see what I was doing, and then they all went off to get their bus, while I followed the crowds back to the station for the train back to Brussels. On the way back into town my phone rang (with its *Great Escape* ringing tone!) and it was Mel, back in Northallerton. I had a quick word with him, then Jane (his girlfriend), and then Chris (another Darlo fan from Northallerton, who is strangely proud of being a fraction Scottish!). They were all as happy as fuck, but not as happy as me because I was there in Charleroi.

After speaking to them I got through town, passing a mob of press gathered around a car with its windscreen put through, at which point I shouted, "Germans did that!" and made my way to the train station.

At the station a crowd of about 50 people had gathered waiting to go through the entrance. It was difficult to see what was happening at the front, but as the crowd doubled in size it became apparent that the police were only letting people in a few at a time. By the time I got near the front, through one set of doors but before another where the police were, it was as crushed as fuck in there. Bloody hot as well. People pushing from the back didn't exactly help the incompetence of the police. Why the hell were they restricting us going through like that? It was stupid.

But anyway, once through I went to the platform where most people were stood, and after several contradictory announcements from two conductors on the platform as well as the tannoy system, it turned out that the train that had been sat there for ages was actually the one for Brussels. I got on the train and managed to find a seat, but by the time the train finally started to move the train was well packed and people were stood on just about every square foot of floor space.

The journey was a nightmare. It was boiling hot on that train, and the open windows did little to resolve the problem. My voice was also completely fucked again after a week of drinking, smoking and singing, so that ruled out any conversation with the others around me.

After about an hour we stopped at Brussels Midi station. Most people got off because nobody knew if the train went on to Brussels Central where most people wanted to be, and not many people knew where Brussels Midi was, except that it was in Brussels. Outside the station one lad was walking back the other way, and said, "Good luck lads, there's hundreds of Turks all tooled up waiting for you down there, just take care."

"Fucking hell, this'll be fun," I thought.

There was a seemingly endless line of riot police, not letting anyone deviate from the main road. I said to one of them I wanted to find a taxi from the front of the station, but he just replied, "No taxi, go that way." Wanker.

After a while we were away from the police, and surprise surprise, after a few hundred yards, some Turks appeared from one of the side streets and tried to have a go. They soon got chased off though. With me being on my own, but within a group of about 200 slightly spread out English fans, I decided to keep near plenty of others and not go off on my own, tempting though it was to batter a solitary Turk stood nearby at one point. When a few more Turks turned up and got chased off, loads of riot police suddenly turned up.

Rather than get caught between two mobs of riot police, I got near to the front of the crowd before the police could block off the street. I soon realised that I was on the main street that led to my hotel, and after the police blocked off the main road further down, I just walked through them with a couple of others, cautiously walking up to one of the Belgian scum bastards and telling them that my hotel was just down the road. For the last quarter of a mile I was on my own, and although there were a few other English about at the bar I'd started drinking at earlier in the day, I went straight into the hotel.

I just knew that the police would be arresting English people all night, whether they had a reason or not, and with me now in charge of two rucksacks, I couldn't risk being nicked myself. I wasn't so bothered about the Turks, because with the numbers of English about, it wouldn't take much to have the Turks on the run even if they were tooled up. But it's like the police set the whole thing up to arrest more of us. Take us to a train station where not many people are sure of the way back to the centre, force us all to go down a long straight road, disappear, wait for the Turks to turn up, wait for the instant English retaliation, block off the road and arrest more English. Just to repeat myself from the previous day's chapter, fucking Turkish scum, fucking Belgian scum.

Anyway, back in the hotel I watched *Match Of The Day* for a while, cheering as they replayed Shearer's goal against Germany, and then fell asleep to the sound of singing and sirens outside. I'd be leaving Brussels the next day, escaping to France.

Day Nine
Sunday 18th June

(Matt)

I WOKE UP on one of the benches at about 8.00am. My t-shirt was covered in sweat so I must have managed a few hours sleep. Most people were laid out on the floor while some had managed to sleep while still sitting upwards on the benches. As everyone gradually woke up, we just waited for an officer to turn up and give us some information. We waited and waited, but nobody bothered to come.

The last 36 hours had been a horrible experience, but the worst was yet to come. At around ten o'clock the drain in our cell started to overflow with piss. Fucking panic. As it all came streaming out of the two small holes in the ground we all got out the way by standing on the benches. If it had happened an hour earlier then it would have soaked everyone who was asleep on the floor. All the blankets were still on the floor so they got ruined.

We were all going mad and calling for someone to come through and take a look at what happened, but it took about ten minutes before an officer turned up. The cell could have been on fire and we would just have been left there. He didn't seem to be too concerned about what he saw either. He just had a quick look then fucked off and didn't come back.

I couldn't believe that they were just going to leave us there. At first when the drains overflowed, I was glad because surely it meant they couldn't keep us in their any longer. But they did, the rotten bastards, they kept us in a cell where the floor was covered in piss. If you went to a zoo and saw animals being treated the way we were then you would bring in the RSPCA.

More than ever now I thought I was on the point of an anxiety attack. When I was first arrested all I was worried about was being deported. Now I didn't care if they deported me. In fact I wanted them to. All I wanted was to get out of that cell. In the cell opposite I saw the Villa fan who I spoke to on the Friday night. The one who guaranteed me that we were not going to get deported. He was a happy go lucky sort of character, but by now he looked like a broken man. As did so many others. Even the ones who were kicking off with the Turks didn't deserve this treatment, let alone those of us who did fuck all.

One lad who didn't look too effected the day before was starting to look in a bad way. He looked distressed and kept on saying, "I can't take this no more." Like the rest of us what was bugging him most was the lack of information coming through. They weren't telling us anything, and it felt like we were never going to get out at all. He said, "I don't care if they tell us they're keeping us here until Wednesday after the Romania game, just as long as we know where we stand." I personally would have gone mentally insane if we were to be kept in as long as Monday morning, but I knew what he meant.

All the people in one of the smaller cages at the front had been moved out and replaced with the non English prisoners. I couldn't believe they were still being held. Surely once it was known that they were not English, they should have been released. They were all being held together. There were two Norwegians, two Canadians, four Swedes, and one Pole. The Swiss lad who was still with us went to join them as well.

Two officers then came through, one with our usual diet of waffles, the other with a bucket of soapy water with a cloth in it. He left it in the cell then walked off. What a joker. They wanted us to clean the floor with that! They were really starting to take the piss now.

Not long afterwards a short bald man with a grey moustache came walking down the aisle. He was wearing a white shirt so was of higher rank then most of the officers. We wanted some answers out of him. The little fucker gave us the silent treatment. He was smiling and looked like he was mocking us. Someone asked him to give us a reason why we were being held, to which he replied, "Drinking, you were drinking."

That just raised tempers even more. If drinking was a crime in Belgium then what the fuck were they doing serving alcohol? And what about the Belgians themselves, as if they don't drink, they're famous for it. If they couldn't accept the fact that we want to come to their country and have a drink then they shouldn't bother hosting major tournaments in their shitty little country. Plus the fact that when I was arrested I was stone cold sober.

A few lads in the cell were beginning to think that we might end up being charged. Then people started to worry about things like, if we plead not guilty then they might keep us detained for longer. Some innocent people were considering pleading guilty just so they could get out of the cell and back home as soon as possible. I couldn't see them charging us though. They just wanted us out of their country, problem was they weren't doing a very good job of it.

A new Norwegian was added to the cell that was full of the non-English prisoners. He was wearing a Norway top and started to go a bit mental. He started shouting, "I am Norwegian, I'm not English, why are you keeping me here?" And "You bloody English hooligans you ruin it for everyone."

He started kicking the cell, then tried to climb the cage which was a bit pointless bearing in mind there was a ceiling. A few English went up close to the cell and told him to shut the fuck up, but you can't blame him for acting like that. It was interesting that the ones who told him to keep his mouth shut were the ones who were kicking off on Friday night.

Another lad who was in the cell opposite started to go a bit mental as well. He was shouting out things like "Fucking sort it out yer useless twats," "You don't know what the fuck's going on," and "Your country's fucking shit, you fucking Belgium cunts!"

Sentiments echoed by the rest of us. I felt like going mad myself but I made an effort to keep it all in. It's amazing how some people can stay calm and relaxed in such a situation. Some people even managed to sustain a sense of humour and I don't know how. There was one lad from Sheffield who every now and then would just casually sit up and say, "Right, starting to take piss now."

I needed to get some fresh air badly. It was hot inside the cell and there was no ventilating machine to cool things down. And of course there was the lovely aroma of piss in the air. I asked a couple of the officers if they could let me out for a few minutes to get some fresh air, but they refused. All requests to see a doctor were also ignored. The floor was covered in litter by now, mainly empty packets of waffles and bags of water. The best thing you could do in there was put your t-shirt over your head and pretend that you were somewhere else. By the time it had reached 4.00pm, we had been in that cell for over 30 hours. Some had been in even longer.

Finally an officer came down and told us that we were being moved upstairs to a bigger cell, and that by the evening we would all have been sent home. I wasn't going to believe them until they opened the cage door and let us out, but for once they kept to their word and led us down the aisle and on the way to slightly better surroundings. Being in that cell was one of the worst experiences of my life and to get out was such a relief.

Out of the four cells the only group of people to stay put were the group of non-English prisoners. As I walked passed them I asked the Polish guy who I spoke to on the Friday what was going to happen to them. I couldn't believe it when he told me that they were going to be deported back to their own countries. And there was me thinking that they would be released when it was found out that they were not English. Whoever was in charge of making the decisions had a very fucked up way of looking at things.

The cell upstairs was three times the size of the previous one and had a much higher roof which made it feel less claustrophobic. It was still a complete dump, but it felt good to get out of that other hellhole. It was made of concrete and obviously wasn't very comfortable, but at least we all had a little bit more room. Altogether there were about 60 of us inside that cell.

At 6.00pm the British consul finally turned up. As he came to our door, the lad who sounded like Denzel went up to him and said, "We've been asking for you."

The consul immediately recognised him and said, "Oh, I should have known I'd see you in here. How are you?"

To which Denzel replied, "Fine, it's good to see you, where the hell have you been?"

They were acting like good friends. He'd obviously been arrested in Belgium on more than one occasion, most notably in Ostend during France 98.

The consul looked stressed and said that he'd been up since 7.00am trying to sort things out. He had made demands that we all get a hot meal, a shower, and said that they had made a complaint to the Belgian authorities about the conditions we were being kept in. He was particularly disgusted at the horseyard that we spent Friday night in, and called our current cell a disgrace.

We told him that it was alright compared to what we'd just been in, but he said that it was still not good enough. And he was right. It's like saying that you don't mind being given a broken arm because its not as bad as having a broken leg.

He said that the problem was that the Belgium authorities did not have the facilities to deal with such large numbers of people. Fair enough, but then what were they doing sweeping up so many innocent people off the streets if they then couldn't deal with it? Stupid bastards.

We asked him if there was any trouble in Charleroi. He told us that there had been some of the worst scenes he'd ever seen involving English football fans and that UEFA were threatening to throw England out of the tournament. It all sounded pretty bad.

Before leaving the cell, he told us that we were going to be expelled from Belgium, not deported. The difference being that we were only banned from entering Belgium for the remainder of Euro 2000. The temporary ban would also apply to Holland. That was a close one. I'm so glad to be allowed back into Belgium again after Euro 2000. What a thrill.

The flights back to England would be arriving at either Heathrow, Stanstead, and Manchester. It would just be typical if all the Northerners were sent to the Heathrow and Stanstead and all the Southerners sent to Manchester. I asked them to sort it out in a way that would be convenient to all of us, but they weren't interested.

Not long afterwards, names and prison numbers were being called out for people who were going to be sent to the airport. I was waiting for my name to be read out, but it didn't happen.

Half of our cell was cleared which left around 30 of us in there, and I spent the next couple of hours talking to some Hull City and Chelsea fans. For some reason we were then moved to an identical cell just down the corridor. The time had gone 8.00pm and there was only one more flight that was scheduled to take us all back. We were starting to think about the possibility of being kept in another night. After all, we were told by the police that they hoped that we would be sent home tonight. Hoped, they weren't definite, and after all that had gone on the last two days. I wouldn't have put it past them to keep us another night. And as for that hot meal and shower that was requested by the consul, we knew that we wouldn't be getting either.

About 15 new prisoners who had been arrested on the Saturday night were added to our cell. They all seemed to know each other and the way they were acting it was clear that they had come over just for the fighting. They had only been in our cell about ten minutes when their names and numbers were read out as people who were going to be flown home. As they were leaving the cell the rest of us just accepted the fact that we were not going to get home before Monday. They had kept us nearly 48 hours so to be given another 12 to 15 hours was certainly not beyond the Belgium authorities.

Then a few minutes later a load of officers came back and started to read out some more names. Finally they called out what I'd been waiting to hear for ages.

"FIFTY SEVEN, MATTHEW BAZELL."

I couldn't get to the cell door fast enough. Once I'd proven who I was by giving them my home address, they gave me back my bag of possessions and took me downstairs to be signed out. There was a man sitting on a table downstairs who had some papers where I had to sign my name a couple of times. He was also surrounded by about 15 guards. It would have a good opportunity to call them all a bunch of Belgium faggots, but I didn't want to risk being sent back upstairs again. I asked them how it was that they were sending home Saturdays prisoners when there were still lads upstairs who had been locked up since Friday, but they didn't have an answer.

A few lads tried to have a joke by saying things like, "Thanks for having us, we'll make sure we come again," and "We'll recommend this place to all our friends," but the pigs remained stone faced.

It was then time for the handcuffs to be put back on before we got led out to one of the two police buses that were outside. Eventually most people from my cell were being led out, but there must of been some that were left behind. Sitting next to me was one of the four Huddersfield fans who lived in Holland. He along with the other three were going to be deported back to England, with no passport, no bank cards and two hundred Dutch guilders. He didn't have a clue what he was going to do once he returned to Blighty.

The bus soon set off and we were on our way to the airport. This bus had see-though windows so as we were driving through the suburbs of Brussels we could see people on the outside looking at us in fascination. It reminded me of how the people of Warsaw looked at us when we drove though their city the year before for the game against Poland. The only difference was that we were not prisoners then, although by the looks on the Poles faces you wouldn't have known it. It's got to be said that apart from the area around the Grand Place, Brussels is a complete shit hole of a city.

As we passed a large roundabout with a fountain in the middle, we saw some outstretched arms moving around through the water. It could only be England fans doing *Dambusters*. As they saw us drive by they stopped what they were doing and gave us a round of applause. At least someone liked us.

After about an half an hour's drive from the detention centre, the bus arrived at the airport and parked up near the runway. Then an old Hercules plane pulled in and parked up 30 yards from the bus. It was a funny looking shape and looked like it hadn't been flown for years. It would do well just to get off the ground. After watching its propellers warm up, I wasn't looking forward to getting on, but being flown back to England on a war plane would be a fitting end to the whole experience.

We were told that we would be flying into Stanstead Airport, but we would have a 45 minute wait before we could get moving. In that time we watched about 40 plain clothed coppers emerge onto the runway. They would be travelling with us on the plane so for every one of us there was one of them. Paranoid fuckers. That's one of the reasons it had taken so long to deport us. If it wasn't for them we could have been home in half the time. What did they think we were going to do, start a riot on a plane?

One of the coppers was a short, stocky man with a moustache. As I was looking at him, one lad who was behind me said exactly was I was thinking. "Eh, that looks like the bastard that arrested me."

A few other lads seemed to be under the same impression. It can't have been the same guy who arrested all of us, so that pretty much sums up what half the Belgian riot squad look like. The other half look like Jap Stam or Freddie Mercury. Whatever they looked like they were all soft bastards because they hit me with everything they had and yet I never had one bruise or mark to show for it. Apart from my hands but that was down to the broken glass.

After a frustrating wait on the bus, we then boarded the plane accompanied by an officer each. If my hands weren't cuffed I probably would have stretched my arms out and whistled the theme to *Dambusters* on my way. One lad made me laugh when he asked one of the officers what film they were going to show on board. The officer didn't find it very amusing.

To say the plane was cramped would be a bit of an understatement. We were able to sit down, but each person's knees were touching the person in front of them. The same lad tried to get the officer to laugh again by asking, "How's the refreshments lady going to get her trolley through all this?", but he still couldn't raise a smile from the miserable bastard.

The officer who sat next to me was alright, and he gave me some reassurance about my enquires as to whether the plane was safe. He asked me if I was afraid of flying, to which I said I wasn't but it was never to late to start. He then told me that we would be flying to Manchester, as it would be too late to fly to Stanstead because the latest landing time was 10.30pm. The time in England was already 10.00pm.

That was no good for me and about five others, but everyone else came from the north so they were delighted with the news. The five of us who were from the South were fucked as it would be too late to get a train back down to London, plus we never had any English money on us so we wouldn't be able to buy food or even make a phone call.

The flight was rough and I have to admit I was scared. We had not been in the air for long when I decided that I would be absolutely delighted to land at Manchester Airport, as it's a better alternative to landing in the North Sea. Looking back, I think the plane was safe, it just didn't feel like it. I don't think I was the only one who looked nervous either. We had only been up in the air about 20 minutes when the plane started descending in a less then subtle manner. I couldn't understand why we were going down so early. Manchester we were told was over an hour away from Brussels in the plane. That's when I really got worried. It then turned out that the pilot was actually on course to make it to Stanstead before 10.30. Hence the groans from 35 Northerners.

Once we touched down in Stanstead it was a great relief. The brakes on the plane had scared me though as when applied it sounded like something on the plane had exploded.

Our cuffs were then taken off us, and we were led off the plane and finally free of the Belgium scum. As I walked down the runway towards the airport building I had my picture taken by a police photographer. As we were the last fans to be sent home the press had already taken enough pictures of other people so thankfully they had left by the time we arrived. If they had been have there taking photos I would have covered my face up. Not through shame as the press would say, but because it's the natural reaction of someone who's innocent and does not want their face appearing on the front page of a newspaper.

There were a lot of police there though to make sure that we sat down in the lounge and waited our turn to go through customs to be interviewed. Those of us without passports were made to sit separately from the others. A few of the British coppers were being sarcastic twats, but on the whole they were quite laid back. As one of them explained to me, throughout the day they had been on stand by expecting a hardcore element of hooligans to be arriving back. They were very surprised to see that most people who had been deported were just normal lads who were very subdued.

After about 45 minutes, I was sent up to give my details to one of the special officers who was sat down by a table. I never had any identification on me so I just had to tell him my name, address and national insurance number. He wanted to know if I was a member of any football league club in Britain. I thought about it, and decided it was best to tell him that I was just an England fan and didn't support any team in this country. Arsenal have already banned 49 fans from Highbury over the summer and I could do without helping them reach the half century. I didn't have anything to hide, but the problem was that I thought it might be a case of being judged guilty without a trial. I also refused to say whether I was a member of the England Members Club or not.

I had a couple of mug shots taken then had to just sit and wait for everyone else to go through passport control. We were then sent through to the nearby train station and onto a train that was due to arrive in Liverpool Street, in the city of London. No one was charged for the journey, but once in Liverpool Street people would just be left to themselves to find a way back to where they lived.

There would be no trains going back up north until the morning, and even then most people were without money and bank cards. I had heard stories that some people had money stolen from the bags that had their valuables in them when they were in the hands of the Belgium police. It wouldn't surprise me. On the positive side I did hear a story of a Geordie who had to travel back from London to Newcastle by train with no money and no possessions on him. He explained to the ticket inspector that he couldn't pay for the ticket as all his valuables were in Belgium, but would give his name and address so he could pay the fare at another time. The ticket inspector said there was no need to, and said that he could stay on the train, and then wished him all the best. The Geordie said that was the only act of kindness he had received in two days.

I had managed to exchange 1,000 Belgium francs (about £16) for £10 of English money with one lad who had some pounds on him, so I decided the easiest thing to do was to get off at Tottenham Hale and get the underground direct to Finsbury Park. By the time I got to the underground, trains had stopped running so I had to get a taxi back home which cost me a tenner exactly. The taxi driver was a Somalian and he was telling me about how the England - Germany game went. He seemed quite positive about it and was saying how well Keown and Campbell had played in the centre of defence. At least it sounded like things were starting to improve on the field.

After what had gone on the last 48 hours I was glad to finally be back home. What I needed most was a shower, a shave, and to brush my teeth. As far as I knew my family didn't know what had happened, so I thought my mum would be surprised to see me when she opened the door. Luckily though, Jamie had saved me a lot of explaining, and had phoned them to tell them what happened, so when I finally turned up they were just glad to see that I had got home in one piece. They told me that once they found out that I'd been arrested they'd tried to get some information about where I was and what was going to happen to me, but the Belgium authorities couldn't have been less helpful. The British Consulate were very helpful though and so was my local MP. If Jamie hadn't seen what happened it would seem like I had just disappeared off the planet for a couple of days. Especially as I wasn't even allowed a phone call throughout the whole time.

My mum and my sister couldn't believe how upbeat I was and how well I was looking after all that had gone on. In fact I couldn't believe it either. There were times when I honestly thought that I would be very effected by the whole experience. What I couldn't handle was the feeling of claustrophobia inside the cell, but once out of there I felt fine. In fact, I was so relieved to be free again that I was in quite a good mood. I was tired though and I hadn't slept properly since the Wednesday night, so it wasn't long before I decided to crash out.

Well, we started off as four and now we were down to only one. Daz, Mel, and myself were all back in the green and pleasant land, and it was now all down to Jamie to fly the flag out in Belgium and Holland. For a change there was now more optimism on the pitch than there was off it.

There's only one word left to say after the last two days. Bugger.

(Jamie)

I WOKE UP feeling knackered, happy at remembering our win over Germany, then pissed off about what had happened to Matt. After a lengthy lie in, a phone call home and a phone call to the embassy - neither of which told me any more news about what had happened to Matt - I decided to pack my bag (and Matt's!) and leave the hotel.

As I was packing Matt's stuff I noticed that he'd left his passport, cash card and match tickets in his rucksack. I thought he'd had them with him, but as it turned out I could have sold his ticket for the Germany match and made some extra cash. I just hoped he had enough cash on him to get home from wherever he got flown back to.

Baggy phoned before I could summon up the energy to get out of bed, and said they were going to Lille for the day, which is about ten miles from their hotel in Roubaix. He said to phone back when I knew what train I was getting. Once up and packed, I checked out of the hotel and asked the receptionist to phone me a taxi to the station. It was only about a mile away, but there was no way I was walking it carrying two rucksacks.

When the taxi arrived 15 minutes later, the driver was a Turk and was playing some shit Turkish tape that sounded like it was meant to be a stand up comedian. Must've been shit because the driver wasn't laughing. Anyway, five minutes later we got to the station and I gave the driver no tip whatsoever. I just enjoyed the miserable look on his face as he had to count out every shitty little Belgian Franc for my change. I was sick of Brussels.

Once at the station I bought a ticket to Roubaix via Lille, and was told I'd have to change at Tournai. I missed the first train because the train destination board didn't show Tournai on it. I got confirmation from the information desk that I was on the right platform and waited for the next one, an hour later. Just before the train was due, I realised that the destination board showed the name of Tournai in Flemish, and was something like Dornaik. Confused the fuck out of me. Fucking Belgians.

While waiting I bought a hot dog, seeing as all I'd eaten all weekend was a crappy cheese sandwich before going to Charleroi which consisted of nothing but a large slice of bread and a large slice of cheese. After a quick phone call to Baggy, I was soon on the train and on the way to Lille. It was boiling hot on the train, even with all the windows open and all the blinds down, and there was hardly anyone else on the train. After a ten minute wait at Tournai, which is just inside Belgium although I didn't know that at the time, I was on the next train which arrived at Lille Flandres 15 minutes later.

Baggy was waiting for me at the end of the platform and we spent the next five minutes trying to find the left luggage area, so I could get rid of the rucksacks until we got the train back to Roubaix. The strange thing about the train station was that there was about a dozen coppers waiting for my train to come in, then they disappeared after having a good stare at me walking past. Dunno what they were expecting.

We left the station and then went around the corner to the bar where the others were. I knew Andy B and Sour, who'd been in Eindhoven and had also come down to Wembley with us a month earlier, but didn't know the others properly so Baggy introduced me to Andy T and Sean. Andy B had also experienced the delights of a Darlo v Hartlepool derby match a few months earlier, which was a shit match (1-1), but a good piss up. They're all Leeds fans apart from Sour who supports Man U, despite being West Yorkshire born and bred, and Baggy who follows the mighty Darlo. Like Baggy, they're all in their mid to late thirties. I quickly got myself a large beer and settled down for a good piss up with the lads.

It was a good laugh there, sat in the sun, drinking away. It got too hot though and we all moved into the shade, except Sour who was lapping up the sun. After a couple of hours Darren turned up, a Leeds fan from South London who the others had met the previous day. He was crashing at the hotel in Roubaix and had just been to Brussels South to get his bag which he'd left in a locker there. It was his flag that we'd seen in the square in Eindhoven, the great big 'Motspur Park' one, which he told us is near Wimbledon.

After a cheese sandwich to give me a beer base, me and Baggy went to get the two rucksacks before the office shut at 7pm. It had hardly been worth leaving them there, as we'd only been to the one bar. When we returned Andy T was fast asleep and swaying all over the place, much to the amusement of a bunch of old grannies sat near us. After another beer we decided to move on to find a bar which was showing the evening's football, Slovenia v Spain and Norway v Yugoslavia. We found one about 50 yards away and got the beers in, sitting at a couple of tables near to the front door.

A few lads from Sheffield also came in, a mixture of United and Wednesday supporters, and they were also staying at the hotel in Roubaix. One of them was the spitting image of Rod Stewart, was pissed as fuck and seemed determined to start on anyone. A short while later, a few of the lads suddenly disappeared outside and were chasing someone across the street. Some scummy local North African wankers had approached someone outside and tried having a go, one of them getting some sort of stick from a kebab shop, but they soon got chased off and a couple of them got a slap.

The barmaid was straight on the phone to the police, saying "Les hooligans anglais combatant près de la gare . . . "

French bitch, them bastards started it, not us.

I tried telling everyone to get back into the bar, knowing the coppers were on their way, thinking they'd be less likely to do anything if we were all sat inside. Within two minutes the police were there in numbers, told everyone English to leave the bar, and then surrounded us. I tried to persuade them in French to let us get the train to Roubaix, and although one of them said we could, we were then told we were going to the police station first. Fucking wankers.

A lot of arguing broke out, so a few of the coppers got their batons at the ready. One grabbed me and said "Are you calm?", to which I replied, "Yeah I calm, but I'm fucking pissed off with you cunts."

"Are you calm?" he repeated, this time holding up his baton.

"Yes, I'm calm." Twat.

They then put half of us in one van, then told us to get into another van which had just pulled up, handcuffing us on the way in. I was fucking fuming. We all were, but we knew that if we went mental they'd be even worse with us and would be even more likely to deport us. While we were being nicked, the local wankers who'd started it were stood around laughing, except one who was being taken away to another police station. So two van loads of us (apart from Baggy who for some reason ended up at the other police station) were taken down to the nick where we were uncuffed, taken to a kind of hallway opposite some cells, then handcuffed again in these handcuffs which were attached to the wall. The fucking French bastards.

The police went through the process of breathalysing everyone, which is strange considering none of us was driving. This went on for ages, but after being breathalysed a few people were released, including one bloke, Charlie, who's about 60 and has a pacemaker. After a while, there were nine of us left. I was the last to get breathaylised, after taking a few deep breaths trying to hyper ventilate to hopefully reduce the reading. They took my name, date of birth and town of residence, then asked me to blow into the tube. I didn't breathe as hard as I was making out, and after five or six large beers my alcohol reading showed up as 32mg, which I think would pass a driving breathalyser in England. After that, I was taken back to the bench and handcuffed to the wall again.

We were still not given an explanation as to why we were being held. As we weren't in a cell we still had all of our possessions on us, so I phoned the British Consulate in Brussels, seeing as the number was still on my phone as one of the last numbers dialled. I told them what had happened, and they said they'd contact the British Consulate in Paris. I also asked if they had any news on Matt, and he said they'd still not had any confirmation of his deportation back to England.

My phone also rang a couple of times. First it was Baggy saying he'd been released and was going for the train back to Roubaix, then my brother Dan phoned. He said, "Alright bruv, been nicked yet?"

I told him I had and he didn't believe me. "I'm locked up in Lille police station for doing fuck all."

Then he went off it. "Fucking Belgian bastards . . . who the fuck are they . . . wankers . . . "

"No Dan, Lille's in France, not Belgium."

When the coppers started taking phones off people, I turned mine off and left it in my pocket.

After a while they decided to release Darren, seeing as his alcohol level was lower than the rest of us, as he'd been to Brussels and started drinking later than the rest of us. And then there were eight of us. Me, Andy B, Andy T, Sour, Sean, and three lads from Sheffield. We were getting well pissed off with being kept there, and started whinging like fuck. I noticed that one of the coppers was only about 18 or 19, so I kept calling him "garcon", then "petit garcon" (little boy). The twat just ignored me. Everytime we asked how long we were being kept for they just said they didn't know. They pretended not to be able to speak any English, so I had to speak French to them. You'd think a station full of coppers in a French city less than two hours away from England would have at least one person who was fluent in English.

As we were sat there, a load of non-uniform coppers suddenly came in, dragging some French lad who only looked about 15 years old. He was pushed onto the bench, then one of them grabbed him by the neck, slammed his head against the wall, and kept shouting, "Votre mere est un chien!", which is something like "Your mother's a dog". He was then dragged around the corner, where they gave him a few slaps, then they took him into the toilet, told him to strip, then searched a certain part of his anatomy.

They'd left the toilet door open while this was going on, so for the three of us at that end of the room it was a case of looking away for a few minutes, after which he was taken to a cell, crying his eyes out.

One of the Sheffield lads next to me asked what he'd done, but got the usual reply, "I don't understand."

When I asked him in French he said that the lad had stabbed someone. Suddenly we all felt that the police were justified in treating the little shit in the way that they had. He deserved all he got.

After a few hours there, handcuffed to the wall, we were getting very pissed off and frustrated. There were a couple of cells facing us, both with glass windows, one with one lad in and one with three or four in. Don't know how long they'd been there, but they kept themselves amused by constantly going to the bog, asking for water and trying unsuccessfully to scrounge cigarettes off us.

Sean and Andy T were taken away for questioning for about half an hour, leaving just the six of us there. With the coppers stood around in their office at the end of the room, and boredom setting in, we decided to have a defiant rendition of God Save The Queen, which became louder and louder with each line that was sung. That was followed up by "If it wasn't for the English you'd be Krauts!" It woke up the Frogs in the cells opposite, who seemed quite amused, and even turned the heads of the coppers down at the end.

We were just laughing, somehow smiling despite being in a fucking annoying and helpless situation, still handcuffed to the fucking wall. That little sing-song in custody is one of those moments that will live with me forever.

Eventually, when Sean and Andy T had returned, I started to get some sense out of one of the coppers. After a lot of waffling, he said we could either go into one of the cells until about 4am, or go for a medical first and be let out an hour earlier. A fucking medical?! What the fuck for? We'd had a few beers so they want to give us a medical! Dumb bastards.

The copper then said that we were all going for a medical. As they were looking at our details, including the alcohol readings, they decided that my alcohol level, and Rich's, one of the lads from Sheffield, were low and didn't warrant a medical, so they just uncuffed the two of us and let us go. Fucking weird, after being held for nearly four hours for doing fuck all, they just let me go and crossed my name off their list.

So I picked up my rucksack, and me and Rich went outside as the others were taken off in a van for their medical. As soon as I switched my phone on my parents rang. They'd heard from Matt's mum who'd phoned the British Consulate in Brussels about Matt and had been told that I'd been nicked in Lille. It was just a case of "No, I've not been deported," and "Yes, I'll be fine."

We decided to find the train station, so I asked an old woman walking her dog where it was. She gave us directions, and it was less than a mile away, but we then thought that there'd be loads of North Africans around the station, which could be dodgy for just two of us. We went back into the police station and I asked them if they could phone us a taxi to Roubaix.

They did, and it turned up 20 minutes later and took us to the hotel where I dumped my rucksack in Rich's room. It was then time for some much needed beer, after an unwelcome break from drinking of over four hours.

We walked to the bar where everyone else was, which was only about 300 yards from the hotel. Baggy was there, Darren was there, and also Ginner and Golly, a couple of Baggy's mates who'd also gone down to Wembley on our bus for the Division Three play-off / England v Brazil weekend. There were also about 50 others there who were staying at the hotel and had come with Northern Holidays, and they were all a lot more pissed than me, having been drinking all day without the break of being in police custody. So the next hour or two was spent having a few beers.

On the Friday night in Charleroi, an English lad had been stabbed in the back by a Turk while having a drink outside a bar. The last we'd heard was that he was still critical in hospital, but then Paul from Northern Holidays said that he'd heard that the lad had died and called for a minute's silence. It turned out that the lad hadn't died and was okay, but we didn't know that at the time, and what followed was the most poignant and respected minute's silence since Alf Ramsey had died. It was more like two minutes really, no one seemed to be timing it. I'm just glad that there was actually no need for the mark of respect and that the lad was okay.

I thought that Roubaix would be a nice quiet little French town, with no hassle whatsoever. But all of a sudden, when we were singing *No Surrender* and all the rest, a few dickhead local North African teenagers decided to drive past in their cars, beeping their horns, shouting, and slamming their brakes on. Wankers. Soft as shit. There was no way they'd have a go, they were just trying to wind us up, and it seemed to be working. The barman told us that the town is full of foreigners, and when he closed the bar at about 1am we all walked up to the hotel together, with the odd car full of wankers going past beeping their horn, which was met with a load of verbal abuse.

After what had happened to us in Lille that night, we decided to get inside the hotel and stay there. If the coppers saw us again they would probably nick us and deport us. We went up to the rooms, I got my bag from Rich's room and dumped it in Baggy's room where I'd be sleeping, and went downstairs to see what was going on.

The police were outside and a few people got nicked, so rather than hang about down there, four of us sat around upstairs having a beer in one of the rooms, before going to crash out. I was knackered, so the floor seemed quite comfortable. The other six who'd been arrested and sent for a medical finally came back at about 4am. The doctor said that the level of sugar in their blood was too low, so they all had to eat a yoghourt before being sent back to the cells for a few hours. How bizarre. At least none of us got deported or charged with anything.

Day Ten
Monday 19th June

(Jamie)

I WAS ABSOLUTELY knackered when I woke up in the morning, and felt a bit rough as well. I couldn't be bothered getting up for breakfast, but the other two made it, even though Sour hadn't got back from Lille police station until about 4am. I finally got up at about 11am, and before leaving the room I switched my phone on to check for messages.

Matt had phoned at about midnight, saying he was back home after being deported. I would have had my phone switched on, but whenever you charge your phone up abroad, the battery goes flat within 12 hours because of the lower output from their sockets, which was a pain in the arse. I also got a reply to a text message from my brother Barney, saying he'd lend me some cash and would pay it into my account, seeing as I was rapidly running out of money. Without that I would've had to go home before the quarter finals.

I phoned Matt and spoke to him for about ten minutes, telling him about my weekend and me getting nicked as well. He told me about his shit weekend in the makeshift cells and being flown home in a Belgian Air Force plane to Stanstead Airport (didn't know the soft bastards had an air force, where were they 60 years ago?!). Matt was keen to try to come back over for the quarter finals, so I said I'd post his passport back if I could find a post office. It was good to speak to him after not knowing what had happened all weekend.

He seemed okay, just gutted that he wasn't with us and pissed off at the way they'd all been treated. He also asked if I'd got his jacket which he'd left in the wardrobe in the hotel in Brussels. "Er, what jacket?"

I didn't check the wardrobe, not thinking it had been used, so I'd not found Matt's jacket. A couple of phone calls to the hotel were met with the response that the cleaners hadn't found anything, which really means that they'd nicked it, or the next occupiers had nicked it.

We didn't have anything planned for the day, and we certainly weren't going back to Lille. It would just be a lazy day, wandering around from bar to bar, sitting in the sun (or shade in most people's case), maybe going in the odd shop or two. After getting a drink of water and then orange from downstairs, we went off down the road to the bar where we'd been the night before, sitting outside under a couple of umbrellas. There were nine of us all to together, with Ginner and Golly joining the Lille Seven, when they finally managed to get up.

The first beer was a real struggle, so I went to the food counter at the side of the bar and asked for a bowl of chips. I didn't want much, but what I got was the biggest chip buttie I'd ever seen. Fucking huge it was. A full sized baguette overflowing with chips, probably the equivalent of three of four portions in a chippy back home. There was no way I was gonna eat all that, but with eight helpers, most of it disappeared.

I still hadn't got my appetite back though, and didn't have that many chips myself. I'd hardly eaten all weekend, but just didn't really feel like eating. I was still struggling with the beer though, so my second drink was a coke, which will be hard to believe for anyone that knows me!

Anyway, after about an hour we decided to go for a wander up the road, and after walking for about five minutes we stopped at another bar. The heat was almost unbearable, so with the shade outside the front of this bar not being up to much, me, Baggy and Darren ended up sat inside for a while amusing ourselves with a trivial pursuits quiz machine, which luckily had the option of being in English and also had a World Cup game on it. After Darren went off to find a bureau de change, me and Baggy went outside to join the others.

The thing that irritated me was the amount of locals, especially those of North African origin, who took great joy in staring at us as if we were some sort of zoo animals, which we probably were to them. As we were sat there a car pulled up and four lads piled out (I don't really need to say what their apparent ethnic origin was!), walked over to the bar in a provocative sort of way, came out with some cigarettes, stood about and then fucked off. What was that all about? Buncha wankers. We sort of thought they were gonna have a go and we'd have to kick the shit out of them. They were probably some of those that had been driving past us the night before.

Anyway, once Darren came back we decided to wander off again in search of another bar. We went down another street and came out into a large square, which had a massive old town hall building on one side that was probably the sort of thing that would be of interest to someone who's keen on architecture. In the middle of the square were various things to keep the kids amused, such as a climbing wall, and a couple of small pitches for football and volleyball, both of which were being used.

But then we found what we were looking for, a decent sized bar with plenty of shade out the front. The lads from Sheffield were already in there so we talked to them for a bit. They were already quite pissed, especially the Rod Stewart lookalike. It was dead hot, but a decent breeze had started up so a few of us sat outside in the shade, drinking slowly, chilling out, watching the world go by. It was good there, especially with the breeze, and the beer started to agree with my taste buds and stomach again.

As we were about to move on, Rod the pisshead decides to break his glass on the table. Don't know if it was an accident or not, but with them drinking wine as if it was beer, we decided to try to lose them for the day. I'm not slagging them off, because they were sound enough, but we couldn't be bothered with any more hassle off any coppers, who were bound to appear later on the way they were carrying on.

By now it was late afternoon, so we went for a wander and ended up back near to the hotel, stopping at a bar where there were some of the other lads from the hotel. There were half a dozen of them sat outside, and they were the lads who'd got the bus which picks up in Exeter and London. With no room outside, we had to sit inside, but it was fairly cool in there.

The bar also had a small cigarette counter which had its fair share of visitors. I'm not surprised really, because the girl who worked there was an absolute stunner! She was about 18-19, quite tall and slim, short blonde hair, and was basically a total babe. Best looking French bird I'd seen, that's for sure, nearly as nice as the Dutch bird on the train down from Amsterdam.

It was okay in there, especially with our new found attraction, but then Rod Stewart appears, and the four of them go up to the back of the bar and attempt to play pool. I couldn't see what they were doing because I had my back to them, but I could hear them and they were making right arses of themselves. When they decided to leave, Rod managed to break a marble table on his way out, which made us feel like shit, feeling that we'd get the blame, seeing as we're all English. But as we got up to leave, the barman, who spoke good English, said that there's no need for us to go, we'd done nothing wrong. We just thought that the police would come and arrest the lot of us, but we were persuaded to stay and the police never came to the bar anyway.

So we settled down in there for a few more beers, and ended up playing a lotto type game called Rapido. Basically, you pick any eight numbers from 20, then another number between one and four. A new game starts every five minutes on the TV screen in the bar, and you could win up to 10,000 Francs, about £1,000, which would've been nice. Four numbers were needed for the minimum prize, and then you'd need your extra number to come up as well. We spent well over an hour playing that, everyone picking a number each every time we had a go, but we didn't really win anything.

As sad as it was to leave the gorgeous French bird behind the counter, we left the bar and went off in search of somewhere to eat. We found a Chinese restaurant just down the road, but upon seeing us lot they said that they weren't serving food that night. After a quick look in a Chinese shop opposite, which sold everything from knives to Samurai swords, we ended up back near the hotel at the bar where we'd started off the day's drinking and decided to get some food there.

There were a few of the others from the hotel in there, although there was no sign of the Sheffield lads. Someone said that they'd got nicked and Rod Stewart was being deported. No surprise there, although we later found out that they'd all been released without charge.

The nine of us sat outside, and everyone had steak and chips apart from me, who had chicken and chips, and Golly, who had nothing. The food was nothing special but it was decent enough and the first proper meal I'd had in days.

It could've been paranoia, but we couldn't help noticing the amount of local North African lads driving past in their cars, having a good look at us, and there were also a few sat around inside and outside the bar.

One of the lads from London told us that the hotel owner had said that a couple of hundred local North Africans would be coming down to the hotel and the bar we were in to have a go at us lot. Given the looks we were getting and the amount of them hanging around, this actually seemed believable.

We stayed in the bar for a while, watching Belgium v Turkey on the telly. We decided to get a couple of crates of beer and go back to the hotel later on, but there was still about 20 of us there, so we hung around for a bit. I was becoming restless with all the hanging about, and ended up going in and out of the bar all the time, waiting to see what was going to happen. Fuck all was happening, and the chances were if it was going to happen they'd wait until later on when we were all pissed.

The prompt to go was when Turkey went 2-0 up in the football, and some wankers cheered in the bar. Sean announced that we'd have to go or he'd go off it and do something daft in there. So the nine of us went back to the hotel to drink our cans.

We all went into Ginner and Golly's room, and all the beers were put in a bath full of cold water. It was a very hot night, but it was a good laugh in there, drinking cans of not very cold beer. The Northern Holidays tour would be going back home straight after the Romania match, and assuming that England got the draw that was needed to qualify for the quarter finals, me, Baggy, Sean and Darren would be staying out and the rest would go home. This prompted chants from the four of us of "We're not going home, we're not going home . . . ".

There was some football highlights on, but no one wanted to watch the Turks winning again. The other match was no better, with Italy beating Sweden 2-1. That meant that Italy and Turkey went through from that group, giving us a quarter final against Italy in Brussels. If only we'd beaten Portugal, we'd have been playing Turkey. Now that would be fun! We then heard the news that UEFA would kick England out of the tournament if there was any more trouble from the fans. Gerhard Aigner, the chief executive, said, "UEFA will have to determine whether the presence of the English team in the tournament should be maintained should there be a repetition of similar incidents."

The cheeky bastards. How about kicking Turkey out for the actions of their people in Belgium, and Belgium themselves for being a bunch of useless bastards who couldn't organise a piss up in a brewery. Threatening to kick us out of the tournament was well over the top, but how the press loved it. There was no way they would carry out their threat. If they did, Belgium would be trashed and no amount of riot police would be able to stop the rioting.

I immediately dismissed the threat as a way of providing an excuse for the impending failure of England's 2006 World Cup bid. UEFA didn't want to back England, firstly because they'd put their support behind Germany before England's bid was launched, and secondly because Europe just hates us full stop. Well, that's a slight exaggeration, but it's true in some respects. The threat to kick us out was the perfect excuse that the FA would come out with when they awarded the World Cup to one of the other bidders, who I expected to be South Africa at the time.

We later saw on the news that the Turks had gone on the rampage through Brussels, attacking Belgians and English, and trashing a few bars. Only about 20 arrests were made, and UEFA said that they were just celebrating their victory and there was no problem. The hypocritical bastards. Not just UEFA, but the police as well. If that was England, there would've been 1,000 arrests and we'd have been kicked out of the tournament! Why is it okay for the Turks to trash Brussels and not us?

And still that person who is supposedly our Prime Minister, Tony Blair, apologises to the Belgian government for the actions of the English supporters. I know I said the same thing two years earlier when he apologised to the French after Marseille, but the Belgian government should be apologising to us for the behaviour of their police and local immigrant population. But no, it's always our fault.

Darren and Sean went back down the road to the bar for a bit, and said nothing was happening, and when Darren had a look outside the front later on, he said all there was were a few wankers driving about in cars. A couple of security guards were stood by the door along with four English lads, and whenever the locals stopped at the traffic lights right outside the hotel, they'd sit there with their eyes looking straight ahead, not daring to look at the lads out the front of the hotel. Then when the lights changed they'd beep their horns and shout a load of shite out of the window. Pathetic little fuckers.

Anyway, we finally ran out of beer at about 2am, and were all knackered after a hard day's drinking in the sun, so we all went back to our own rooms and crashed out for the night.

Day Eleven
Tuesday 20th June

(Jamie)

I FELT A bit rough when I woke up, but managed to get up in time for breakfast for a change. Before setting off, I spoke to Matt and arranged for his rucksack to go back on the bus which would stop off at Victoria bus station in London, and he could meet it there in the morning.

I had a funny feeling that I'd also be on the bus though. I just wasn't at all confident about the match. After waiting around outside the hotel for over an hour, we finally set off for Charleroi, with me and Darren scrounging a lift on one of the buses.

The journey lasted for about an hour and a half, and the driver had the same tape playing over and over again, which was mostly crap. One song was okay, *An Englishman In New York* by Sting, which Darren appropriately changed the words to "I'm an alien, I'm a legal alien, I'm an Englishman in Belgium." We were certainly treated like aliens.

When we got to Charleroi we parked up about a mile from the stadium. Our first task was to find the FA's temporary office so that I could pick up my ticket for the match. I asked a Euro 2000 steward and he didn't have a clue. What's the point in employing someone to assist fans when they don't know where something is that turned out to be only 300 yards away from where they were standing?!

I found the FA's little office, after being pointed there by a couple of coppers, and went and got my ticket. The girl behind the counter was absolutely gorgeous, and certainly wins the award for best looking English woman seen at Euro 2000. After getting my ticket it was time to sell Matt's ticket. I sold it to one of the lads from the bus for £50, which gave me some extra cash and got them a ticket at a decent price. After that, it was time to start drinking, seeing as it was now about 2pm and the sun was scorching, so we wandered across the road away from the stadium and went inside a small bar just past an Italian restaurant.

Seeing as there were nine of us we split the rounds of drinks into two groups of four and five. It was 100BF for a large beer, about £1.55, which isn't too bad. The beer tasted good, and was certainly strong, and we spent the next three hours in there, slowly supping away. There was a garage just across the road where I went for a sandwich and some cigarettes at one point.

I was thinking of giving up smoking after the way my throat felt when I woke up, so I'd left my cigarettes in my bag on the bus. Once drinking though, I was soon smoking again and had to buy some more. Couldn't scrounge off Baggy all day. It's funny how only two out of nine of us smoked.

Anyway, going over into the garage was a real treat, as the place was air conditioned and was nice and cool, the equivalent of walking down the freezer aisle in a supermarket on a hot day. We went for something to eat in the Italian place just down the road, where the beer was warm and disgusting, and then went off in search of the main square where Darren had arranged to meet a couple of mates who were brothers. Assuming England qualified, we'd be crashing at their hotel in Brussels.

By now, less than two hours to kick-off, there were loads of people about, especially on the big roundabout with the fountains where we'd been the other night after the Germany match. On the way down to the square my phone rang, and it was Mark, a lad from our office in Nottingham. I'd not met him seeing as I never have to go to the Nottingham office, but he'd e-mailed me at work saying that he'd seen the article in the work magazine about my previous book.

There were nine of them over there, all Forest fans, and they were staying in Ostend (Chapo, another one from the office that was over there, later called themselves "the Ostend Nine"). A few of them had been arrested before the Germany game for not having their passports with them, but were later released, and they were now in the square that we were going to, so I said I'd try to find them. On the way down there, Sean kept stopping to talk to people he knew (is there anyone he doesn't know?!), and when we finally got there I couldn't get through on the phone to Mark so didn't meet up with them. We stopped at a bar just by the edge of the square and had a couple of beers, although by now the warm beer was turning my stomach and I had a bottle of water instead of another beer. Darren managed to find his two mates, so at least we'd be okay for accommodation in Brussels.

With less than half an hour until kick-off, we made our way up to the ground. I couldn't help noticing how different the atmosphere was compared to the other two games. It seemed very low key, almost like a friendly match, and there was a higher proportion of the clowns who go to football in fancy dress, like the four blokes wearing Crusaders outfits that we saw. Baggy made the observation that it was mainly Southerners who were about, compared to the weekend when loads more Northerners were there.

Once through the first ticket check point, I was stood waiting for the others who were buying programmes when I became aware of someone walking towards me from the side. A voice then says in a broad West Midlands accent, "Oi, are you fucking Darlo?"

I looked round and it was Hollis from Wolverhampton, who we'd met at the World Cup and also seen in Sweden, and he was well pissed. It was good to see him again, and I said, "Did you know you're on the front cover of a published book?"

I'd told him in Sweden that I was writing a book about the World Cup, but he didn't know it had been published, so I gave him a flyer with details of the book and also my website, (www.geocities.com/jm_dfc/). He asked where Mel and Matt were, so I told him Matt had been deported for doing nothing and Mel had gone home a week earlier. He also said that there was six of them staying in Amsterdam and they'd be getting the train back there after the match. Apparently there were no trains going to Brussels, only buses, and you had to provide either proof of a hotel booking or a Eurostar ticket back to London. That meant we'd have loads of hassle getting there after the match, so we'd maybe have to think of something else if we couldn't get on a bus.

Hollis then went off to find his mates, and when the others had bought their programmes and stuff, we went into the stadium. I didn't bother trying to find my allocated seat, and just stood in the aisle instead, in a similar place to where I was for the Germany match, this time just behind Hollis. I'd taken my Darlo flag with me, but seeing as we'd arrived about five minutes before kick-off, there was nowhere left to tie it up so I just flung it over my shoulder. I could see Darren's Motspur Park flag up in the main stand, but he must have been told to take it down because it was hanging over the executive boxes and blocking part of the view, and it was gone the next time I looked.

The national anthems were sung, and I was surprised that the Romanian one wasn't booed, but it's a bit different to playing Germany. The match was soon underway, and England had taken over the stadium again, this time on a greater scale with quite a few in the Romanian end. Despite the amount of English there, the atmosphere seemed quite subdued. I just couldn't get the World Cup fixture from two years ago out of my head, when Romania beat us 2-1 after scoring in the last minute. I just had a feeling that history would repeat itself.

The match started off bright enough, but after about 20 minutes disaster struck. Romania, attacking the end opposite us in the first half, went ahead when the ball was crossed and went in off the post. I couldn't believe it. England then played 20 minutes of shite, and just before half-time I went up for a drink. Just as I got my drink of water, a big cheer went up and as I rushed towards the top of the seating area it turned out that England had got a penalty after Paul Ince had been fouled.

Yes. Come on.

I could barely see the goal from where I was stood, inside the stand behind all the seats, but Alan Shearer took the penalty and scored easily to make it 1-1. After celebrating the goal I went for another drink, and as I was paying for it a massive cheer went up and England had scored again, this time Michael Owen hitting the net.

Yeeaass!

We went mental. The ref blew for half-time and everyone was busy dancing around, singing "We're not going home, we're not going home, we're not going, we're not going, we're not going home!"

Things were suddenly looking good. Romania had to score twice to knock us out, and surely that wouldn't happen. But within five minutes of the second half starting, Romania had levelled the scores when a weak punch out from Nigel Martyn in goal fell to one of the Rumanians who scored from the edge of the area.

Bollocks.

Oh well, if the scores stayed as they were in the two group games, we'd still go through. England played crap for the second half, defending too deep and not really creating much. Only Martin Keown seemed to know what he was doing, along with Beckham and Shearer. All through the second half I had a couple of right wankers behind me, constantly slagging off the England team, the Rumanian team, the ref and the linesmen. All they were saying with their whinging Cockney voices were things like "Facking 'ell Neville, you're shit", "That's facking shit Beckham", "Linesman, you cant", "You facking Rumanian gypsy baarstard."

On and on, irritating as fuck.

Even though England weren't playing too good, they seemed to be getting a lot of luck, and I now had the feeling that we actually had a chance of winning the tournament. Either that, or we'd be knocked out in the first round, I just knew it would be one of the two.

Then it happened.

With barely a minute left to play, one of the Rumanians ran with the ball into the penalty area, ran towards the touchline, then with Sol Campbell covering, Phil Neville decides to tackle the Rumanian, but instead brings him down and gives away a penalty. The stupid wanker. He'd been playing shit all night, but now he goes and gives away a penalty in the last minute when there was no need to even tackle.

As I was saying, I started to feel that England were going to go on and win the tournament, which seems quite bizarre now, but I convinced myself that Nigel Martyn would save the penalty and we'd hang on for a 2-2 draw and the point we needed. But no, it wasn't to be, the Rumanians scored to go 3-2 up, and despite a few desperate efforts on goal, England couldn't equalise and we were out of Euro 2000.

Fuck. Fucking bollocks.

Most people were stood in a state of shock and disbelief, while others stormed out of the stadium swearing like fuck.

So that was it. No glory for England, the wait goes on.

No return to Holland. We were going home. After the hassle we'd been getting in Belgium I was almost relieved to be going home, but I was gutted that we were out. If we'd have qualified, we'd just have one more game in Brussels and then we'd be in Holland for the rest of the tournament.

I left the stadium and made my way to the fountain where we'd all arranged to meet up. All around me was a scene of devastation, in sheer contrast to the other night after the Germany match. I'd heard someone say that Germany had got beat 3-0 by Portugal, so that was some consolation, but it didn't soften the blow. We were out, that was that.

Once everyone had arrived we made our way back to the buses. There was no point in staying over there, so after having a word with Paul from Northern Holidays, and paying £35 each, me and Darren got the bus back to London. We were on the other bus this time, not the one with Baggy and all on, but I recognised a few of the lads on it, and talked to the lad next to me who was a Crystal Palace fan.

I was knackered, gutted, and in need of some beer, but we weren't due to get the ferry until 4.45am, so I'd have at least another five hours before I could have a pint. Someone put a weird film on called *The Matrix*, which was okay but became too bizarre and I ended up dozing off for about half an hour.

We stopped at a service station for about half an hour, and because of the huge queue most people helped themselves and walked out without paying. A busload of Rumanians turned up and left five minutes later.

"Probably going to Dover to claim asylum," I said.

We stopped at a cash and carry booze place near Calais, but they weren't letting us in, which Paul wasn't too happy about, so we made our way towards home and parked up with all the other buses. I stood around and talked to Baggy for a bit before we got back on the buses and boarded the ferry.

Seeing as we were the second bus to board the ferry I was near the front of the queue for the bar. At last, a long awaited pint, at four 'o' clock in the morning, English time. There was only one barman serving, and he was slow and useless, but I suppose that's because he was French. When I got my pint it was fucking disgusting. Warmer than all the beer I'd had in Belgium. I only drank a bit of it, then went down to the bar at the other end of the ferry where I found the others in the queue.

Darren bought me a cold can of Grolsch which was much better, and we all sat down near the window, drinking and eating. Darren developed a fixation with the roll down plastic blinds, which had "do not open" printed on them. He was determined to get them open and managed to raise one of them a bit, but all the effort seemed to confuse him because he looked out of the window and said, "That must be the Isle Of Wight!"

Everyone on the ferry was totally knackered, and by the time we got to Dover it was daylight. So I suppose that was the start of the next day . . .

(Matt)

SO MUCH HAD gone on over the last few days that I'd forgotten that there was a football match between England and Romania still to be played. As far as the football was concerned I could take it or leave it. As for the rest of the country, well everyone was on a high after the 1-0 win over Germany. It had lifted the spirits of the whole nation and there was a real sense of anticipation going around for Euro 2000.

Personally I couldn't give a shit. I didn't really feel part of it. My mum had recorded Saturday's game for me, but I don't think I'll ever bring myself to watch it.

I'd spoken to Jamie in the afternoon, and he had some good news for me. Sour and Andy were returning back to England after the Romania game and would bring home my rucksack and passport. Their coach would be stopping off at Victoria in London at around 6.30am so it would be easy for me to meet up with them. If England were to be knocked out then Jamie would be returning on the coach too, but we fully expected to get the result against Romania.

Now that I was going to get my passport back I was thinking about the possibility of returning to Belgium for the quarter final against Italy. I really didn't want to go back to that country, but two things made me think about it. Firstly I had a ticket, and secondly to complete this book that myself and Jamie were writing, it was no good being stuck back in England.

It was going to be hard to return though. The British government had given a guarantee to Belgium that the 900 fans deported would not be allowed back into their country. My passport wasn't stamped, but my details and photograph were now with the police who would be out in force at all the ferry ports and airports.

My plan was to take a cheap flight to Paris then make my way up to Brussels by train where there's no passport control. I thought there would be less checks by the police at passport control for flights to Paris. I would have been travelling by myself which would also be an advantage. Another alternative was to take a ferry to Boulogne. Pretend I was going for a day trip then make my way up to Belgium. After all I was not banned from travelling to France. I was banned from entering Belgium and Holland for the remainder of Euro 2000, but could they legally stop me from entering France?

There was another problem though, apart from the travelling. When I said I had tickets for the quarter final what I meant was I had a voucher that had to be exchanged for a ticket by the England Members Club who were based in Brussels. There was a real possibility that my details had been handed to them by the police and that I could be blacklisted. It was all looking like the whole thing would be too much hassle. I was going to try to get back, but the realistic side of me thought that I'd rather move to Zimbabwe and become a white farmer than go back to Brussels.

Since I had been back in the country, I had read various reports from our wonderful, fair, unbiased, un-sensationalist, open minded, truth hunting, multi-talented media. Written by journalists who do this country proud with their high standard of reporting. In fact they got to me so much that I phoned most of the newspapers up to try to give them the other side of the story.

What really got to me was the fact that they had reported that 900 thugs had been deported from Belgium. We had no trial and had not been charged, yet we were all labelled thugs. Before a murderer or rapist is convicted they are referred to as "the alleged" or "the accused". Some how we don't get that right.

At first I spoke to almost all of the national broadsheets and not the red top newspapers who I didn't think were worth the phone bill. Apart from the *Daily Telegraph*, none of them were at all interested in what I was telling them about my experience over the weekend. The fact is that hundreds of innocent people had been arrested in a foreign country for daring to be English and then been treated like animals in prison. You'd think that would be something that the media in this country would immediately pick up on and take an interest in. After all, they stick up for a British nanny in America who was accused of killing a baby. They also stick up for other Brits who are on death row in America. Yet because we're football fans accused of disturbing the peace, we are automatically guilty, and seen as too risky to stick up for. Wankers.

As I said I wasn't going to bother speaking to the red top newspapers, but one tabloid in particular that day was so full of shit that I felt I had to phone them up. I was put through to a journalist on the newsdesk, and started off by telling him of my experience to see if his newspaper was interested in hearing the other point of view to what they'd been reporting.

At first I was very polite to him, but the man on the other end was just a complete tosser. Typical tabloid scum. He wasn't at all interested in what I was telling him, then started asking stupid questions like, "Where were all the hooligans in Eindhoven?" and "How did you obtain your tickets?"

If I were to answer that, then the next day you would read, "ENGLISH SOCCER THUGS ALLOWED TO OBTAIN TICKETS FROM THE FA". I was just honest with him. I told him that I didn't trust him.

When I asked him how it was the media can say that 900 thugs have been deported when none of us had been charged, he stuttered and had no answer. As he did for most of the conversation.

By the end I'd had enough of him. And I seem to remember the conversation ending like this.

"I'm disgusted at Tony Blair. If he's going to apologise to the Belgium government, then the Belgium government should apologise to us for wrongful arrests of hundreds of Englishmen"

"Of course Tony Blair had to apologise. What happened in

Belgium was a disgrace to our country."

"Your newspaper's a disgrace to are country"

"Oh so what happened in Charleroi was the media's fault?"

"I didn't say that."

"Yes you are, blaming the media for all that's gone on."

"I'm not talking about the football. I'm talking about 365 days a year. You're a disgrace to our country every single day. I'm talking about the way you treat people in general. You and the other tabloids."

"You're blaming the media for all the trouble. You're blaming everyone but the hooligans."

"Don't put words in my mouth. Were you in Brussels?"

"You blame the press, you blame the police, you blame the Turks, you're blaming everyone apart from the hooligans. You're talking out your arse"

"You're a prick."

He hangs up.

Good because I'd had about enough of talking to him. What a tosser. If that's the kind of man that writes for our national newspapers, it's no wonder British journalism is in the state that it is.

I also thought that the news coverage on the television was totally one sided and biased. As I was watching one of the reports, I noticed they were interviewing the Chief of the Brussels police force. When asked if he thought his police force had arrested too many people he responded with, "No, I don't we arrested too many people, I don't think we arrested enough people."

Anyway, for the Romania game I joined my brother, Tim, and a few mates in a pub called the Boston Arms in Tuffnell Park, North London. I found it really difficult to get into the game, and as I sat there watching the big screen all I could think about was that I should be there in the stadium. It was very depressing. I could hardly cheer the team on, and never felt nervous when Romania were on the attack.

When England scored I raised a couple of half hearted cheers. I had about as much enthusiasm for supporting my team as your average season ticket holder in the west stand upper at Highbury. I was watching everyone around me acting how I would normally act when England were playing. I didn't care if we won or lost.

That was until we conceded a penalty in the last minute. The realisation that we were about to fuck it all up once again brought me back to my normal self.

"You wanker Neville, you fucking wanker. I knew you were

gonna fuck it up for us! Come on Martyn, save it please . . . "

When Romania scored, I just stormed out of the pub. I couldn't believe it. It was all over. Unlike previous tournaments we didn't even go out with any pride.

As we were stood outside the pub I saw some wanker celebrating. He was some wide boy in a suit, and was clenching his fists going "Yes, fucking yes!" whist waving around a betting slip. I've never been so tempted to hit someone in all my life.

Problem was I was in the business of clearing my name so the last thing I needed was an assault charge that was related to football. I settled for just letting him know that he was a cunt. I was hoping he would do something back, but he just walked across to the other side of the street. With any luck someone chinned him later on that night.

As everyone else went home, myself and Dave, a fellow Gooner, stayed back and drowned our sorrows in the Boston Arms. Our frustrations were taken out on *The Sun* plastic hats that littered the pub. I must have crushed at least ten of them. I was gutted, but in some ways I was quite relieved that it was all over and that I wouldn't have to worry about going back to Belgium. And at least my bank balance had something to cheer about.

I had to wake up early the next day to meet Jamie at Victoria station so I left the pub and made my way home. Dave stayed behind and was on a mission to drink himself unconscious in some late night pubs in Camden. It was the same pub and the same walk home as it had been from four years ago when Germany knocked us out of Euro '96. I have to say though I wasn't half as upset as I was when the Germans beat us.

When I got back to the house I watched a *Panorama* documentary that I recorded from BBC1 that night. The programme had secretly followed England fans around at Euro 2000, from Eindhoven to Charleroi. I have to say that I thought the whole programme was total garbage. All it showed was a few nasty characters, who we all know travel with England anyway, so really the programme uncovered very little.

They had claimed it had been a violent eight days which was untrue as the only violence was on the day of the Germany game, and the night before in Brussels. Because there was no trouble in Eindhoven they decided to make a big deal out of the chant, "No surrender to the IRA!" My own opinion of the song is that it's a bit pointless as the IRA do not have a bombing campaign going on anywhere in Britain at this time, and I don't think that following

158

football should become that political. But at the end of the day it's a song against a terrorist organisation so really what's the big deal? It's being made out that the only people who sing *No Surrender* are hooligans which Is totally untrue. It's also somewhat hypocritical of the press to criticise England fans for singing "No surrender to the IRA!" when they say exactly the same thing in their newspapers after every terrorist atrocity.

Panorama also made the Turks and North Africans look like innocent victims. When over 1,000 of them went on the riot after the Turkey v Belgium game, *Panorama*'s excuse was "Violence breeds violence, England fans must realise that what they see as fun is deeply offensive to other communities."

WHAT?!

These people make programmes on current affairs. Surely someone must have informed them that two Leeds fans were murdered in Istanbul by a mob of Turks who had the intention to kill. After that incident you'd think that the Turks would keep a low profile, but no, the night before the UEFA Cup final in Copenhagen they attack a pub full of Arsenal, outnumbering them five to one and stab another Englishmen. The next day in the main square, Arsenal have a go back at the knife merchant scum and get all the blame. As a Gooner I never felt any shame whatsoever for what happened. As *Panorama* would say, violence breeds violence.

And of course not once did that programme show the tooled up gangs of local Turks and North Africans of Brussels who were out to fight with the English and deserve at least 50% of the blame for what happened.

But anyway, after watching that garbage I soon crashed out in the sad knowledge that once again we'd been let down on the football pitch by our national team. We couldn't even feel any pride in our performance either. Oh well, it's a shame, but Euro 2000 hadn't really ended on a very happy note.

Day Twelve
Wednesday 21st June

(Jamie)

ONCE WE'D DOCKED at Dover, we got back on the buses and then stopped at the bus park just through customs. A few people were getting off at Dover, and Baggy and the others also had to change onto our bus, which would take them back up north.

Once on the move again and onto the motorway, the *Blackadder Goes Forth* video was put on, but I fell asleep within five minutes. When I woke up the video was still on, but the signposts were saying "Central London 15" instead of "London 55". I must have managed about an hour's sleep, but was still knackered.

We finally arrived at Victoria at about 6.30am, and most people got off the bus. With me carrying two rucksacks, me and Darren walked down the road to the bus station, which is where I'd arranged to meet Matt. Darren went off to get the tube and Matt turned up 20 minutes later. "Last time I saw you, you were getting nicked!", I said to him. We then got the tube and a bus to Matt's house in Crouch End.

After exchanging tales of being arrested in Belgium and France, I watched the *Panorama* programme about the England fans at Euro 2000, which was a load of bollocks, and dozed off for a few hours. We went out in Finsbury Park later on, met Darren, watched the Holland v France game which the Dutch won 3-2, got pissed and went back to Matt's. I went home the next day, feeling absolutely knackered, gutted that we were out, but content in the knowledge that I'd had a good time and had completed another tour of duty with the army of St George.

Conclusion

(Matt)

WELL, ENGLAND PLAYED shit, France won, and I got deported from Belgium and missed the Germany game. What else is there to say? Well quite a bit actually.

There's a few things I'd like to get of my chest, and I think I'll start with the British media. Firstly they glorify brash behaviour on one hand, then condemn it on the other. As do a lot of the British public. Rock bands are glorified when they trash a hotel or get into a punch up, yet when football supporters act in the same way they are seen as the scum of the earth. British holiday makers in places like Ibiza are also seen as a good laugh, but from what I can make out, they're more of an embarrassment to our country than any football fans.

The Sun always talks tough on crime. So then why do they sponsor *Lock Stock* on TV? A good programme, but one that blatantly glamorises criminals. They also encourage sexist and laddish behaviour, yet are up in arms when someone has an affair.

The fact was that the media's coverage on the trouble at Euro 2000 was sensationalist and completely over the top. Before the tournament they were predicting deaths in Charleroi. Yet from what I've seen on the TV, the worst trouble In Charleroi was when about 50 lads started throwing chairs along with the Germans and a police van came in and fired a water canon at everyone. It's the same footage they show every time. Yes, it was not a very nice incident, and of course it should be reported, but I thought the media coverage that followed it was just out of all perspective.

The Mirror says that there should be a minimum prison sentence of five years for the worst offenders when it comes to football violence. Now I'm not sticking up for football hooligans, I thought some of the people who I saw in Brussels on the Friday night before the Germany game were complete meatheads who I've got no respect for whatsoever. But five years? Would you get a five year prison sentence for starting a fight outside a pub or a club? What's the difference? Muggers and rapists don't even serve five years. Of course they should be punished, but sentences should reflect the seriousness of the crime, football related or not.

The media also blame hooligans for England's failure to be awarded the 2006 World Cup. But they have to ask themselves, what did they ever do to support our bid? All they did was slag it off and undermine it in every way possible. I wonder if the media in Germany and South Africa were as hostile to their respective bids as we were to ours. My personal opinion is that the right wing aspects of the media had their own political agenda. For this country to host the World Cup would have looked good for the Labour Government, and I think that if Tony Blair had not been as supportive of the bid then the media would have backed off a little bit more. It had got to the point where even the murders of the two Leeds fans in Istanbul was used as a weapon to undermine our chances of hosting the tournament.

In terms of the 2006 World Cup, it would have been nice to see it come to this country, but I don't mind them giving it to Germany. At least it means I'll be able to afford to go. South Africa's too far away to travel. I know people say that it should go to an African country, but when you look at it, the north African countries are closer to Germany than they are South Africa.

As for our bid, I think that we would have given ourselves more of a chance if we had made it a British World Cup bid instead of an English one. We could have asked the Irish to join us as well. Venues like Hampden Park, Ibrox, Celtic Park, the Millennium Stadium in Cardiff and even Lansdowne Road would have made it a much stronger bid. Plus just the presence of Scotland, Wales, and Northern Ireland would have made FIFA less hostile towards us. It's no use crying over spilt milk though, we'll just make sure we have a good time in Germany instead.

Another thing that I'd like to get of my chest is Jack Straw (not literally of course). He says he wants to redefine what it means to be English! What people like him have to understand is that the more they try to impose political correctness onto people, the more people will lean in the other direction. He's his own worst enemy. When he tells us that we're a jingoistic violent race it just adds to our resentment because we know that it's not true.

I also think that his new laws on travelling football supporters are totally unfair and against civil liberties. I've got no problem with him wanting to ban known hooligans from travelling abroad, but under these new laws a lot of innocent people will be victimised. You cannot stop people from travelling abroad to watch England because you suspect that they might cause trouble. It's a very dangerous route to go down, and where do you end up drawing the line? It will all be left in the hands of officers at passport control who could start turning people away for a tattoo that they're not sure about, or for a minor offence that has nothing to do with football.

The Tories are full of crap as well. The way they go on you would think that football violence was a new problem, and that nothing ever went on between the years 1979-1997. They had 18 years to take out legal injunctions on known trouble makers who travel abroad, yet they did nothing, so really they should keep their mouths shut on this subject. As should most people who no nothing about football, but still decide to make outspoken comments about it. I think that's what winds me up the most, when Mr and Mrs Milton Keynes express their outrage at football supporters when they know nothing about the situation whatsoever.

One man though who makes all our politicians look fair minded is our good friend, the Mayor of Brussels. My personal vote for biggest knobhead of Euro 2000. When 1,000 local Turks and North Africans went on the riot in Brussels he decided to blame the English! Apparently we provoked them. If that man hadn't given them an open ticket to riot then there wouldn't have been half the trouble there was at Euro 2000. He openly admitted that he didn't want any Turks or North Africans to be arrested because they would have to live with them after the tournament. Arresting as many English as possible was not a problem because we could just be deported.

The situation between English fans and certain immigrant populations of Europe is starting to become a big problem. It's the equivalent of Belgium or French fans coming to watch a football match in England and being attacked by a mob of Pakistani locals. It wouldn't happen, but if it did then I'm sure this country would take some responsibility for it. To me the whole thing illustrates the large racial tensions countries like France and Belgium have with their immigrant populations and it is seen as politically insensitive to arrest them. This whole problem is likely to continue unless the local immigrant populations are threatened with the same treatment by the police as the English are. As long as they've got an open ticket to riot then it will continue for a long time.

I have to say the whole thing has turned me very much against the European Union. The bottom line is that after the way I was treated by the Belgium authorities, I never want them to have the opportunity to have a say in my life ever again. The European Union is supposed to be big on human rights, yet where were the basic human rights of those of us stuck in a detention centre in Brussels, the very heart of the EU?

I wrote to my MP explaining what happened and basically asking for some sort of explanation as to how the Belgium authorities were allowed to get away with treating us the way they did. She then passed my letter on to Lord Bassam, a Home Office minister, who responded with this feeble reply.

"I recognise that being caught up in such a volatile situation must have been extremely worrying for Mr Bazell and all concerned. I can assure Mr Bazell that the Government, police, and the FA are all committed to doing what they can to ensure that decent law abiding supporters travelling abroad to watch their team are able to watch football in a safe and secure environment. We have extensive experience of dealing with football hooliganism in this country and took every opportunity to share our expertise with the Belgium and Dutch authorities prior to the Euro 2000 tournament. At these meetings, the Belgium police made it quite clear that they would pursue a policy of zero tolerance towards any outbreak of disorder during the tournament. As Mr Bazell will appreciate, it would not be appropriate for any Government minister to comment upon the tactics used by the Belgium police.

However, English football supporters must accept that the policing tactics and tolerance levels experienced here will not always apply overseas. It is vital therefore, for supporters to ensure that their behaviour is not perceived as offensive or provocative by local people or threatening by local police, and that way avoid potential troublemakers. It is clear from Mr Bazell's letter that he was detained as an "administrative arrest" under Belgium public order legislation and that no charges were brought against him. It may be of some comfort to him that in this case there is no scope under present legislation for a banning order to be brought against him."

I appreciate the fact that he bothered to reply, but really the letter is just a patronising cop out. Why would it be inappropriate to comment upon the tactics used by another country's police force when the European Union makes legislation which affects this country and are particularly hot on human rights? Especially when the Belgium authorities violated basic human rights. I'm not asking them to do a Lord Palmerston and start a war on another country for an Englishman who's been arrested, but it's about time somebody high up started to stick up for us.

The final thing I'd like to get off my chest is the Belgium riot police. During the 1998 World Cup I remember thinking, "Is there any group of people that I dislike more then the French riot squad?" The answer is yes. They're called the Belgian riot squad. To put it simply, they're just a bunch of violent Nazis. The brutality they demonstrated to those of us who were arrested was on a different level. It was as if they had something to prove.

In recent years, the Belgian police have received a lot of criticism from their own country over the way they handled cases such as the infamous paedophile ring, and of course the Heysel stadium disaster back in 1985. A source who works in Belgium has told me that he thinks that these things may have been a factor in the way they went about things in Euro 2000.

As far as the football goes, I have to say that the French were definitely the best team and deserved to win the competition. I did feel quite down though after the final because I was watching another country win, and I felt that it will probably never be England in that position.

From England's point of view it was the worst showing in a major tournament since Euro 92. Hopes were never really that high from the start though and when you look at it we were lucky just to be there. Maybe the fact that we usually get knocked out of international competitions with a certain amount of pride has stopped us from changing the way we play the game in this country. Perhaps after this feeble showing we might now have a serious look at the way we coach young players.

I've got a lot of respect for Kevin Keegan, but I think he's just too tactically naive to coach at the highest level. When was the last time England conceded three goals in one game, let alone conceding six goals in three games as was the case in Euro 2000? Even though in the past we've never been very successful, England have always had a good team. This time though we were just very poor and didn't even go out with any pride. I suppose we gave the neutrals a bit of entertainment though, as our group games against Portugal and Romania were two of the most exiting of the tournament. I wouldn't call that much of a consolation though.

I do think that this country deserves a bit of sporting success. In football more than other sports because the fans are thanklessly loyal to a team that consistently lets them down. The best thing we could do would be to start afresh and bring in a lot of the decent young players that are coming through at the moment. Players like Paul Ince and David Seaman have been brilliant for England, but it's now time to replace them and start all over again.

Anyway, despite the way things ended I would say that travelling to Euro 2000 was still well worth it, and we still had a good time especially in Eindhoven. The Dutch deserve a lot of praise for the way they went about things and they were perfect hosts for the tournament. Wonder what Japan and South Korea will be like in the 2002 World Cup? Who knows, we might win it. Then again Spurs might win the league, Ian Paisley might turn Catholic, and Anne Widicombe might feature on the front page of *Playboy* (sorry if I just caused widespread vomiting with that last one). Oh well, keep the faith. COME ON ENGLAND, COME ON ENGLAND!

(Jamie)

THIS WAS THE first time since 1992 that England had been knocked out of a tournament because we were shit. In 1998, we went out of the World Cup in France on penalties after being cheated by Argentina and a dodgy ref in the second round. In 1996, we went out of the European Championships in England on penalties to Germany in the semi-finals, after playing well and missing a few chances that would have won the game for us. In 1994, we didn't qualify for the World Cup in the USA after a the German ref changed his mind about giving a penalty against Holland and didn't send off Koeman for a professional foul, and he later scored. And Graham Taylor was clueless.

In 1992, at the European Championships in Sweden, we were shit. And Graham Taylor was clueless. In 1990, at the World Cup in Italy, we went out to Germany on penalties in the semi-finals, after playing well and nearly winning it. In 1988, at the European Championships in Germany, we were shit, losing all three games. In 1986, at the World Cup in Mexico, we got cheated out of the tournament by a cheating Argie spic scoring with his hand. In 1984, we didn't qualify for the European Championships in France. In 1982, at the World Cup in Spain, we didn't get beat, but went out in the second round group phase. But at Euro 2000, England were shit.

On the football side of things, the only good thing was beating Germany. At last, after all these years, we've beaten the Germans and made them look even shitter than we are. Let's just hope we can repeat the results in the 2002 World Cup qualifying campaign. And at least we were there, after our feeble showing in the qualifying group.

But what bothers me about both those things, is that we'll end up becoming like Scotland. They're shit and they know they are, and are just happy to qualify for a tournament and follow it up with the usual first round exit. And beating England is the most important thing in the world to them. They didn't care that they didn't qualify for Euro 2000. They beat us at Wembley in the second leg of the play-off and that's as good as winning the tournament for them.

England beat Scotland to qualify and we beat the Germans. But it should be more than that. For the first tournament in years, I really struggled to have any belief that England would win it. It's only the fact that I'm generally optimistic (I have to be, following Darlington) that gave me any hope for England's chances at Euro 2000. We should be winning tournaments, but yet again another competition ends in disappointment.

England were going places under Terry Venables and he came so close to getting us the long awaited glory at Euro 96. Glenn Hoddle seemed to be carrying on the good work at first, but then things went downhill and he lost the plot. Under Keegan, we've not really done anything. England are looking more like the team of 1992 under Graham Taylor, and that's certainly not the way to be going.

Keegan has the respect of the players, fans and media, and he should be given a chance, but he's tactically naive and lacks the experience of coaching abroad that Venables had. He should maybe bring in some decent coaches to help out, people with experience of football around Europe. He also needs to bring in some younger players, like Rio Ferdinand, Joe Cole and Frank Lampard of West Ham, and Steven Gerrard of Liverpool who played well against Germany.

Something needs to be done. Playing with a 4-4-2 formation would be preferable, but when England use that formation it's just too predictable and we get caught out. We've played the best football in recent years with a 3-5-2 formation, although that's never perfect. Ideally I'd have Venables back in charge.

In terms of attending the tournament, I'd had a good time over there, but it had been a tale of two countries. Holland was great, Belgium was shit. The Dutch seemed so chilled out and welcoming, whereas the Belgians were just like you'd expect for the home of the European Commission, with the authorities being well over the top. In Eindhoven and Amsterdam, the police wandered about in plenty of numbers, but we rarely saw any in riot gear, and they kept their distance from us even when we got a bit boisterous, if that's the right word.

In Brussels and Charleroi, riot police were the order of the day, and as soon as more than ten English people were together and sang a song, the police would be straight in there. I have to say though that despite slagging off Belgium, we had no trouble from ordinary Belgian people. Or the French in Lille and Roubaix. They were generally fine with us. I don't mean this to sound racist because it isn't, but the only problems at Euro 2000 were where there were large groups of immigrants from Africa or Turkey. This was pretty much the same as in the 1998 World Cup in France, where the only real problems were in Marseille.

What happened to Matt was well out of order. Like hundreds of others who were arrested, he did nothing to even warrant attention from the police, let alone be arrested and deported. If standing in a street, not saying a word, not even drinking alcohol, makes someone a hooligan who is a disgrace to the country, as our politicians and media suggest, this country is fucked up.

People at home make these statements without the faintest idea of what actually happened or what it's actually like to follow England abroad. They see a short clip of a few chairs being thrown on the telly and then launch a scathing attack on anyone who's English and is attending the football.

They see a group of lads singing *No Surrender* and label us mindless scum. But what exactly is wrong in singing a chant of loyalty to the patron saint of England, and also a chant of defiance to a terrorist organisation that has killed and maimed innocent British citizens for several decades, and is still in possession of a huge arsenal of illegal weapons and still carries out "punishment" beatings amongst its own community?

These politicians and media do far more damage to England than anyone who was at Euro 2000. In my opinion, they are just ignorant scum. But it makes me wonder. I know what I saw happen at Euro 2000, and I know of the contradictory reporting of events back home. So what else in the news is a complete distortion of the facts? Probably more than anyone dares to imagine.

Apart from the reporting of England football fans abroad, there's probably nothing more distorted in the media than the issue of the United Kingdom's membership of the European Union. Now I know it's not football, so I won't dwell on the subject. I disliked Brussels enough before I went there, seeing as it's the home of our masters, the EEC. Now I hate the place.

Our country, if it can correctly be defined as a country now, is being ruled by Brussels. They impose laws upon us and overrule our own laws. We are in Europe and ruled by Europe. The EU has its own foreign policy, social policy, agricultural policy, fisheries policy, monetary policy, the list is endless. Politicians on the continent openly state that the single currency is just a step to the political union of Europe.

Our government wants to sign up for this, handing over control of monetary policy to the European Central Bank in Frankfurt, leading to tax harmonisation (i.e. tax increases), and yet they still say that giving up the pound is a purely economic issue. I urge everyone to vote NO when we finally get a referendum on the single European currency.

The UK is a global country, with trade links all over the world. We are the biggest foreign investor in the USA. We have £1,900 billion invested around the globe. We have the world's fourth largest economy. The UK should leave the EU, replace membership with a free trade agreement, negotiate a free trade agreement with the North American Free Trade Agreement (NAFTA - USA, Canada, Mexico), and make our own laws for our own country. We should pursue trade links with the Commonwealth. We do not want to be a part of the Federation of Europe. In the words of Winston Churchill, "We are with Europe, but not of it. We are linked but not combined. We are interested and associated but not absorbed."

And after the way we were treated in Belgium (and France), there's no way I want them bastards interfering any more in my life.

Something else that annoyed me shortly after the tournament was Jack Straw, the Home Secretary, slagging off England again. Not the football team, but England the country and the English people. He said, "There is a particular problem with some people's view of Englishness. There is a distorted, incomplete idea of what it is to be patriotic for those in England, which is different from that in Wales or Scotland or Ireland. We've had all the global baggage of the empire and a lot of jingoism here. And I think it's very important that we redefine not only what it means to be British, but also what it means to be English. I am proud of not only being British, I'm also proud of being English. But I am also pretty worried that others try to capture and distort this definition. It is the responsibility of people who have a leadership position in our society, like me, to try to change that."

What an absolute wanker. How can he say he's proud to be English when he wants to change the very essence of being English? If he hates being English so much, he should fuck off to Brussels and live there. Given his pro-EU opinions, it seems that he wants England to exist only as a geographical area, divided up into regions making up part of the European Empire. He's the one with the problem on what it means to be English. What's wrong with being proud of a nation's history?

The Americans are proud of their declaration of independence from Great Britain. The French are proud of their revolution and their evolved identity. The Scottish are proud of fighting off the English 700 years ago, and are proud of their own identity. So why is it wrong for us, the English, to be proud of fighting off invaders for over 900 years, stopping the likes of Napoleon and Hitler from taking over the whole of Europe? We stood alone against the Nazis in 1940. It's a long time ago now, but so is Bannockburn and the Scots have enshrined that victory at the heart of the identity. I don't hear Jack Straw criticising them.

And as for the Empire, it wasn't perfect, but it gave us trade links across the world that are still strong today. And without the Empire, the English language would not be spoken as widely as it is. It also helped less developed nations across the world to build up their industry and infrastructures. And when the time came to move on we peacefully established a Commonwealth from it.

Jack Straw singles out English patriotism for being different to that of the Scots, Welsh and Irish. People of those three nations show their pride by saying how much they hate the English. And Straw is defending that? He calls us jingoistic? A few months earlier he had said that the English are "potentially very aggressive, very violent" and will increasingly express their Englishness because of devolution. He also said that the English had used their "propensity to violence" to "subjugate Ireland, Wales and Scotland. Then we used it in Europe and with our Empire, so I think what you have within the UK is three small nations in terms of their population who've been under the cosh of the English."

Excuse me, but the Act of Union between England and Scotland was voluntary, and has benefited Scotland enormously over the last 300 years. What an arrogant wanker the man is. He is right in one sense though. If people like him keep making these remarks, keep destroying our country, and keep telling us to be ashamed of our country, we may well become very violent and rightly so. Any other nation would react the same way to the amount of shit that we now have to take in this politically correct "new Britain".

As for his football hooligan legislation, he's going well over the top. He wants to stop people from leaving the country merely on suspicion of going to cause trouble. 99% of those that follow England abroad may be viewed with the potential of getting involved in violence. Not many actually do, but giving a copper the right to stop a British citizen from leaving the country, merely on a suspicion, is a plain breach of human rights.

If he wants to stop trouble abroad he should stop slagging us off for being patriotic. Going abroad to watch England is one of the few places where it's okay to outwardly show pride in being English. And yet the media and politicians want to stop this because they are afraid of patriotism. Being proud to be English doesn't fit into their idea of politically correct new Britain in the European Empire. Well they can all fuck off. I'm English and proud of it, and I will not surrender to the EU or anyone else who wants to take away our identity.

Anyway, back to the football. Shortly after the tournament finished, FIFA announced who will be hosting the World Cup in 2006. The five bidders were England, Germany, South Africa, Brazil and Morocco. UEFA gave their backing to Germany, who were the original European bidders for the tournament, so with all but one of the European FIFA executives stating their intention to vote for Germany, things looked doomed for England's bid from the start.

Confidence began to build up in the bid though, and it seemed at one point that we'd be in with a chance of hosting the tournament. South Africa were the favourites, especially after the FIFA president, Sepp Blatter, openly declared his support for their bid. Now there's impartiality for you. There would have been fears about safety in South Africa, but I'd be okay for accommodation with cousins in Johannesburg, Durban and Cape Town. As for Brazil and Morocco, they had no chance really, and Brazil pulled out a few days before the vote.

On the day it went down to a final vote between South Africa and Germany, and when Charles Dempsey, the New Zealand representative, abstained from this final round of voting, Germany won by 12 votes to 11. So after spending £10 million on the bid, England lost and the World Cup 2006 will be in Germany.

The FA had their perfect excuse, blaming England fans at Euro 2000 for everything, especially with UEFA's threat to kick us out giving them ammunition. The truth is that we had no chance anyway, after the FA broke an alleged gentleman's agreement to support Germany after we received support to host Euro 96.

Only two of the 24 man FIFA executive promised to back England's bid, both of them Jocks, although one emigrated to New Zealand in the 1950s. Another three agreed to vote for England in the second round so the FA didn't get too embarrassed. But the FA didn't do themselves any favours by constantly slagging off everyone else. They've done more to harm the image of English football than any of us who were at Euro 2000.

Looking on then, we've got World Cup 2002 in Japan and South

Korea, which I'm tempted to go to. Then it's Euro 2004 in Portugal, which will be okay. Then World Cup 2006 in Germany. Things will go off in Germany if England qualify, especially with all the Turks that live there, if events of April to June 2000 are anything to go by. I'll be 33 by then, don't know what I'll be doing, but will probably go. I can see it now. "For you, zie World Cup ist over. Your cell ist second left, third reich!"

I said before the tournament that if England didn't win I'd have liked Holland to win it. Once England were out, the Dutch were the only team I wanted to win it, seeing as we'd had such a good time there and the Dutch people had been sound. The other teams I wanted to do well, Norway, Sweden, Denmark and the Czech Republic, all went out in the first round. It was good to see Turkey get beat, but when the Dutch went out after missing four penalties in the semi-finals, two in open play and two in a shoot out, we were left with the worst possible final, France v Italy.

It was a total non event for me, as they were the two teams I least wanted to win the tournament out of those that had a chance. I have to admit though that France are the best team around at the moment and deserved to win, and it's always good to see Italian football players and fans looking devastated.

Ten years ago, France were the laughing stock of Europe, they were shite, while Germany were winning everything, or certainly challenging for everything. Now it's Germany who are shite, and France are winning everything. It's bad, having France as the World and European Champions, but no side looks better at the moment.

But me being the eternal optimist, I think we'll qualify for the World Cup in 2002 and go on to win it, or at least reach the semi-finals. No matter how shit England are, me and thousands of others will never lose the faith, and will always enjoy supporting England in the belief that one day we will finally live the dream and experience well and truly, England's glory.

Come ahead if you think you're hard enough . . .

Terrace Banter was launched in October, 1998, as a football imprint of S.T. Publishing. Over the past decade football as a spectator sport has changed beyond all recognition, particularly for the ordinary fan. A great deal of working class culture and tradition is being cast to one side so that football can appeal to a new market, that of the "soccer fan".

Through Terrace Banter we hope to put down in print the experiences of the ordinary fan before they are lost forever in a sea of plastic seats and replica strips. Unless we document our own history, it is left to outsiders and the mass media to be judge and jury.

We are interested in hearing from authors who have written or are writing a football book that they think would find a home at Terrace Banter.

Even if you don't think you can write the book yourself, we can help you get your words into print.

You can write to us at

Terrace Banter
P.O. Box 12
Lockerbie
DG11 3BW
Scotland

www.terracebanter.com

info@terracenbanter.com

Available now from Terrace Banter

St George
In My Heart

Confessions Of An England Fan
by Colin Johnson

"It heats the blood whether you're with him or running in the opposite direction."
Sport First, April 2nd, 2000

When he's not on domestic duty with Millwall, Colin Johnson spends his time and money following his beloved England over land and sea. And not as part of the official travel club either. Here's his account of trips to Scotland, Italy, Ireland, Wales, Poland, Czechoslovakia, Sweden, Spain, Holland, and of course Wembley before it became populated by happy smiley people chanting "Football's coming home".